THE GUIDE TO
THE RIGHT TO MANAGE

SUZIE SCOTT
DAVID CLAPHAM
ANN CLARK
ROBINA GOODLAD
HILARY PARKEY
DAVID RODGERS
MALCOLM WILLIAMS

THE GUIDE TO THE RIGHT TO MANAGE

CONTENTS

CHAPTER 3
FEASIBILITY STUDIES & DEVELOPMENT PROGRAMMES

CHAPTER 4
MODULAR MANAGEMENT AGREEMENT

CHAPTER 5
SELECTING AN AGENCY

CHAPTER 6
WORKING WITH AN AGENCY

CHAPTER 7
ESTABLISHED ORGANISATIONS

APPENDICES

ACKNOWLEDGEMENTS

THIS GUIDE WAS COMMISSIONED BY THE DEPARTMENT OF THE ENVIRONMENT AS PART OF THE GUIDANCE ON THE RIGHT TO MANAGE. IT FORMS PART OF A SERIES OF BOOKS AIMED AT HELPING TENANTS TO SET UP TENANT MANAGEMENT ORGANISATIONS.

THE PROJECT WAS A COLLABORATION BETWEEN RESEARCHERS AT THE UNIVERSITY OF GLASGOW AND PRACTITIONERS FROM TPAS (SCOTLAND), CDS (LIVERPOOL) AND CDS (LONDON). THE SUPPORT OF THESE ORGANISATIONS IS ACKNOWLEDGED.

THE INFORMATION ON CONSTITUTIONS WAS ADAPTED FROM WORK CARRIED OUT BY ESTHER GOULDING AND NEAL PURVIS FOR TPAS (ENGLAND).

HELPFUL COMMENTS ON THE DRAFT REPORT WERE RECEIVED FROM THE PROJECT ADVISORY GROUP OF TENANTS, LOCAL AUTHORITY OFFICERS, AGENCY WORKERS AND SPECIALISTS. TEAM MEMBERS ALSO RAN A NUMBER OF WORKSHOPS AT CONFERENCES AND SEMINARS ON THE APPROVAL SYSTEM FOR AGENCIES AND THE MODULAR MANAGEMENT AGREEMENT.

THE SUPPORT TEAM WHO HELPED TO PRODUCE THE GUIDE WERE BETTY JOHNSTONE, WHO TYPED THE TEXT; PAUL HERMANN WHO TOOK THE PHOTOGRAPHS; SHAUN ASKEW, WHO PRODUCED THE LINE DRAWINGS AND ROBERT STRAIN, WHO CO-ORDINATED AND PRODUCED THE LAYOUT.

FINALLY, THE TEAM WOULD LIKE TO THANK THE TENANT PARTICIPATION BRANCH OF THE DEPARTMENT OF THE ENVIRONMENT FOR ADVICE AND SUPPORT THROUGHOUT THE PROJECT.

CHAPTER 1
INTRODUCTION

BACKGROUND

THIS GUIDE to the Right to Manage has been written to provide advice about developing a tenant management organisation. It is aimed primarily at tenant readers but can be used as effectively by local authorities and training agencies.

The Guide is part of series of books about the Right to Manage. It provides an overview of the process while others give advice about specific things.

The guide will help you to:

- **Understand the Right to Manage process**

- **Use the modular management agreement**

- **Select and work with an agency**

- **Work as an established TMO**

WHAT IS A TMO?

TENANT MANAGEMENT is a form of participation in which the tenants in an area take on the responsibility for day-to-day management and repairs. The council still owns the property and tenants keep their secure tenancy.

To take over management, the tenants must set up a properly constituted organisation - *a tenant management organisation (TMO)*.

The responsibilities of the council and the TMO are negotiated and set out in a management agreement.

TMOs may take different forms. They all have to be incorporated, either as an Industrial and Provident Society, or a company.

They each have a committee or board, elected by members, which oversees the management of the estate. People with specialist skills may be co-opted onto the board to offer particular knowledge or experience.

Tenant Management Co-operatives

Some TMOs take the form of a co-operative. These are often called Tenant Management Co-operatives. All tenants in the area can be members of the co-operative.

The management committee usually is made up just of residents. Local authority representatives or councillors may be on the board but in non-voting posts.

Estate Management Boards

Other TMOs prefer more of a partnership with the council. Here there is more emphasis on tenants and council representatives working together.

These organisations are often called *Estate Management Boards*. The board is made up of tenant representatives, councillors, and other co-opted board members, although tenants are always in the majority.

WHAT DO TMOs DO?

SOME TMOs decide to take over most of the day-to-day management of their area, while others concentrate on particular functions.

TMOs can decide to take over only a few responsibilities at first and increase them later, once they are more experienced and established.

Typically, a TMO will be responsible for:

- **Letting the houses to new tenants**

- *Day-to-day repairs and maintenance*

- **Cleaning and caretaking**

- *Dealing with neighbour disputes*

- **Collecting rents and chasing arrears**

- *Ensuring the tenants are informed and listened to*

- **Employing staff to carry out these functions**

- *Managing and controlling the budget for management and maintenance*

The TMO will negotiate an allowance from the local authority for management and maintenance of the properties.

The size of this budget is usually determined by the number of properties to be managed and the services which the TMO provides.

Samuda, Isle of Dogs

HISTORY OF TENANT MANAGEMENT

THE FIRST tenant management organisations were set up nearly 20 years ago after a clause in the *Housing Rents and Subsidies Act 1975* allowed local authorities to hand over management of estates to tenant management co-operatives.

Initially, this form of management grew slowly, but in the mid-1980s, the government introduced grants to pay for training and support.

Funding

Following a review of funding arrangements in 1988, a government report *Tenants in the Lead* (DoE, 1989) recommended increased funding and training for trainers' courses.

By 1994, there were 74 established tenant management organisations and a further 88 tenants' groups were well down the road to taking over management.

WHY TMOs ARE SET UP

THE IDEA OF setting up a tenant management organisation can come about in a number of ways.

In some areas, the local authority may suggest the idea, in others tenants may hear about TMOs and decide to explore the idea further.

Better way

There are a wide range of reasons why councils and tenants are interested in tenant management.

Many councils encourage tenant participation and management because they feel that this is a better way to run housing services.

Improvements

In some cases, the council wants to carry out major improvements in an area. They must get permission to spend from central government and this funding approval comes with the condition that tenants on the estate are consulted and involved.

Tenants who set up TMOs may also be interested because they want to see the houses and the area improved:

> *'Seeing the houses being improved ... wouldn't have happened if we hadn't got involved, because you need the tenant participation to get the allocation money from the government.'*
>
> *Board Member - TMO*

Some tenants' main interest is to get better services, particularly for repairs.

> *'We figure that no matter how badly we do, we can do better than the council.'*
>
> *Board Member - TMO*

For tenants such as these, tenant management actually works. It allows them more say in the running of their homes, with the benefit of the ownership of their estates staying with the council.

The government believes that these opportunities should be available to all tenants and so has introduced the Right to Manage.

Legislation

The legislation to give this right was included in the *Leasehold Reform, Housing and Urban Development Act 1993* and came into force on 1 April 1994.

Tenant management organisations, which have been approved by the Secretary of State, do not fall within compulsory competitive tendering arrangements.

THE RIGHT TO MANAGE

FROM 1 APRIL 1994, tenants' organisations who have a constitution which demonstrates that they are representative and accountable can exercise the Right to Manage.

It can take two to three years to set up a tenant management organisation, from the initial idea to taking over responsibility for managing the area.

Involvement

During this time, your group will have to make a lot of decisions and get involved in a wide range of activities.

The Department of the Environment divides the Right to Manage process into 3 main stages:

1   Promotion:

Getting the initial ideas about tenant participation and the different options for control. Setting up a tenants' organisation with a constitution and deciding to exercise the Right to Manage.

2   Feasibility
(or initial feasibility):

Appointing an agency. Looking at the options for greater involvement in more depth. Beginning to learn about housing management, equal opportunities and management skills. Carrying out a ballot to find out whether residents support the idea.

3   Development
(or full feasibility):

Deciding what sort of TMO you want and which functions you want to manage. Drawing up policies and procedures. Negotiating a Management Agreement with the local authority. Holding a final ballot. Setting up systems, appointing staff or agents and taking over management.

WHAT THE GUIDE CONTAINS

HOW DO WE GET STARTED?

CHAPTER 2 outlines the promotional stage and the things that you need to do when you first start to think about tenant management.

This includes adopting your constitution, getting support from members and serving a Right to Manage notice.

WHAT IS INVOLVED IN FEASIBILITY & DEVELOPMENT STUDIES?

CHAPTER 3 outlines the jobs that are involved in the feasibility and development stages, explains how your *'competence to manage'* will be assessed and how you can get funding for the support and advice you will need.

WHAT IS A MANAGEMENT AGREEMENT?

ONE OF THE MAIN tasks at the development stage is to negotiate a management agreement with your local authority.

Chapter 4 explains how the management agreement works and outlines how the TMO will be paid for the responsibilities it takes on.

WHERE CAN WE GET HELP AND SUPPORT?

BECAUSE THERE is so much involved in setting up a TMO, you need someone who can provide advice and support.

Some local authorities employ tenant participation officers or co-operative development workers who may be able to help you.

Guidance

But even if you get good support from your council most groups feel that they need independent guidance.

The Department of the Environment has an approved list of agencies who have a lot of experience in working with tenants.

Chapter 5 outlines how you can go about choosing an agency to help you and Chapter 6 describes how you can make sure that you work in partnership with an agency.

WHAT HAPPENS AFTER THE TMO IS ESTABLISHED?

ONCE YOUR TMO has taken over responsibility for managing the area, you need to manage the organisation.

This involves recruiting and working with staff, making decisions, making sure that the TMO is providing a good service and keeping within budget.

Chapter 7 outlines how you can ensure that the TMO is working well.

HOW TO USE THE GUIDE

READING THE Guide will give you some idea of what is involved in developing a tenant management organisation. Different bits of the Guide will be useful to you at different times.

The contents page, and this introduction, should help you to find the sections you need to look at in depth.

Information

There are also a number of other books, produced by the DoE, which will give you more detailed information. These are mentioned in the chapters and listed at the end of the guide.

New Barracks, Salford

CHAPTER 2
Getting Started

INTRODUCTION

THIS CHAPTER takes you through the things that you need to do when you first start to think about tenant management. This initial stage is called, *promotion*.

What you need to do during the promotional stage, and how long it takes, will depend on the starting point of your group. The key tasks are:

- **Getting information about the options for control**

- *Finding out how the housing service works and what the problems in the area are*

- **Setting up a tenants' organisation**

- *Adopting a constitution*

- **Getting the support of your members**

- *Serving a Right to Manage notice*

If you are in a tenants' association which has been running for a while you may already have done most of these jobs. But if you are a group which has just got together you will need time to get organised.

You may also need some support and advice. The book *Learning to*

Manage gives more information on what you need to know and suggests some training sessions you may find useful.

Council support

In many cases, your local council will help you to get going. The majority of local authorities support tenant participation in the management of their homes and will encourage and support tenants' groups.

You may also be able to get independent advice and support from an agency.

Funding

The Department of the Environment provides funding to a number of organisations to promote tenant participation and tenant management and will be able to give you a list of agencies.

If you don't have support from your council or an agency at this stage you can still exercise the Right to Manage. The rest of this chapter tells you how.

ADOPTING A CONSTITUTION

ONCE YOU HAVE got a small group of tenants together who are interested in tenant management, one of the most important things that you need to do is to adopt a constitution.

The constitution is important. You cannot be recognised as a TMO unless you have a constitution which meets the conditions set by the Secretary of State.

Under the Right to Manage legislation only tenants' organisations who have met the requirements for a TMO have the right to request the Right to Manage the housing in their area.

The key conditions that your constitution must include are that:

a) **The area covered must be specified**

b) **Any tenant (including any secure tenant) in your area may become a member of the organisation**

c) **It is made clear that the organisation will avoid discrimination on the grounds of racial origin, gender, sexuality, disability or religion in anything it does**

d) **The business of the organisation is decided and organised either through the membership at general meetings or by a committee or board of directors elected by the membership**

By following these principles you can ensure that your tenants' organisation is democratic, representative and accountable. In addition, you must show that at least 20 per cent of tenants in the area are members.

Geoff Gillan chairs a meeting, Foxhole TRA group

If you do not meet these conditions, your local authority can refuse to accept a Right to Manage notice and the Department of the Environment will not provide funding for the next stage.

DRAWING UP A CONSTITUTION

A MODEL constitution is set out in *Appendix 1.* You don't have to adopt it, but it will be of help if you need to draw up a new constitution or amend an existing one.

The usual things a constitution will cover are noted in the checklist below:

Checklist - Clauses for Your Constitution

- **The area to be covered**
- *Your organisation's name*
- **The aims of the organisation**
- *Equal opportunities*
- **Who can be a member**
- *Meetings*
- **The Committee**
- *Standing orders*
- **Office bearers**
- *Co-opted members*
- **Financial control**
- *Providing information to members*
- **Winding up the organisation**

DECIDING THE AREA

THE FIRST THING that you need to do is to decide on the area which your organisation will cover.

Longshoot Estate, Haslingden

If your group has been a tenants' or residents' association for some time you may simply take your existing geographical area.

For the purposes of the Right to Manage, the properties must be within one local authority area and geographically defined - not scattered at random round different parts of an area.

Numbers

The minimum size is 25 council-owned flats or houses which are occupied by secure tenants. There is no maximum size laid down - some existing TMOs cover 2,000 homes.

You need to think about what would make sense for the TMO to manage and how local residents see the area.

You should show the area you have defined in a map which is attached to the constitution.

CHOOSING A NAME

MANY TMOs use the name of their estate or area. This has the advantage of being recognised but, if the area has a poor reputation, you may want a new name to show that you intend to create a new image.

AIMS OF THE ORGANISATION

THE AIMS should set out who you represent and what you want to do. The model constitution sets out a number of aims. These include:

✔ **Promoting membership**

✔ *Promoting equal opportunities*

✔ **Improving the housing service**

✔ *Promoting social, welfare and training activities*

✔ **Representing members**

✔ *Consulting members*

✔ **Monitoring the organisation**

✔ *Providing training*

You need to make sure that the constitution covers all the things you want to do.

EQUAL OPPORTUNITIES

IT IS ESSENTIAL that your constitution contains a clause on equal opportunities. The model constitution in *Appendix 1* gives three alternatives which would be accepted.

WHO CAN BE A MEMBER?

YOUR CONSTITUTION should make clear who can become a member and how people can join. As a minimum you should make membership open to all local authority tenants and leaseholders in your defined area.

You can encourage younger people to get involved by allowing all residents over the age of 16 to become members.

Records

You must keep annual records of membership to show your support. This can be done through an application form or a membership book.

You also need to decide whether to charge a membership fee. If you do charge a fee it should be small so that everyone can afford it.

Campaigning

Because you need to show that 20% of the tenants in your area are members, you are likely to need to get people to carry out a door-knocking campaign to explain what the organisation is about and persuade people to join.

Organising social activities can also be a useful way of promoting membership.

ENDING MEMBERSHIP

THE CONSTITUTION also needs a clause about how membership can be ended.

This would usually be when someone moves out of the area (so that the organisation cannot be controlled by non-residents), ceases to be a tenant or leaseholder or for gross misconduct such as racist, sexist or threatening behaviour.

ANNUAL GENERAL MEETING

THE ANNUAL General Meeting (AGM) is important because it ensures that all members have the opportunity to find out what is happening, elect committee members, and vote on resolutions.

The AGM should:

✔ **Present an annual report**

✔ *Present audited accounts*

✔ **Appoint an independent auditor**

✔ *Elect a committee*

✔ **Consider any resolutions put forward by members**

✔ *Vote on any resolutions*

✔ **Vote on any amendments to the constitution**

The constitution should include a clause stating that members will be given written notice of the AGM and detail when resolutions will be accepted.

THE COMMITTEE

SOME VERY small TMOs manage to run their organisation without a committee. Instead, decisions are made by the membership at general meetings.

However, most TMOs find that they need a committee to run the organisation.

To show that the organisation is democratic and accountable, the committee should be elected at an Annual General Meeting.

Numbers

The constitution should specify the number of committee members and the minimum number of committee meetings which should be held each year.

You will also need to give the committee the power to create sub-committees or working parties.

STANDING ORDERS

THE STANDING orders are the rules governing the conduct and procedures of committee meetings to help you conduct business efficiently.

The constitution need only make provision for these - you can draw up the details separately.

11

OFFICE BEARERS

THE CONSTITUTION should set out which office bearers the committee will have and their responsibilities. As a minimum you should have a Chairperson, Secretary and Treasurer.

Many tenants' organisations have additional posts such as Vice-Chair, Assistant Treasurer, Minute Secretary and Publicity Officer.

This can help to spread the tasks around committee members and make sure that everyone plays an active part in the organisation.

CO-OPTED MEMBERS

YOU SHOULD HAVE a clause which allows you to co-opt people onto the committee.

This can be used to fill places if committee members stand down, to bring in people who can provide specialist knowledge or to make sure that particular groups are represented.

PROVIDING INFORMATION TO MEMBERS

MAKING SURE that people know what is going on is vital if you are to retain support. Information is also an important first step to participation.

The constitution should include clauses confirming that the tenants' organisation will provide information, including minutes of meetings and copies of the constitution.

Languages

You should also think about providing information in other languages, if there are residents whose first language is not English, and recorded tapes for people who are unable to read.

FINANCIAL CONTROL

KEEPING GOOD control of money is important for any organisation. The constitution should detail how this is to be done.

WINDING UP THE ORGANISATION

YOU NEED A clause on what happens if the membership wishes to dissolve the organisation.

Usually this is done by calling a special general meeting at which decisions on the disposal of any assets will be taken.

PUTTING BASIC SYSTEMS IN PLACE

During the course of drawing up your constitution, you will have put a number of basic systems in place which will help you to run your tenants' organisation. These are detailed in the checklist below.

Checklist
- Basic Systems for Your Organisation

- **Has a list of properties been drawn up?**

- *Has a map showing the area covered been set out?*

- **Are up-to-date membership records kept?**

- *Have 20 per cent of the tenants in the area become members?*

- **Has a committee been elected?**

- *Have office bearers been appointed?*

- **Have standing orders been drawn up?**

- *Has a bank account been opened?*

- **Have cheque signatories been agreed?**

- *Has an independent auditor been appointed?*

- **Are minutes of committee meetings kept?**

- *Do all members have a copy of the constitution?*

In addition to checking that your constitution meets the conditions on page 8, your council may also want to check that you have these systems.

GETTING SUPPORT FROM MEMBERS

ONCE YOU HAVE adopted your constitution, you need to decide whether to request the Right to Manage. The decision must be made democratically.

In order to find out if your members support this proposal you need to do one of three things:

- **Vote on a resolution at a General Meeting of your organisation**

- **Carry out a door-to-door survey of members**

- **Carry out a ballot of members**

You need to show both that a majority of tenants (including leaseholders) who are members support the proposal and that a majority of secure tenants who are members are in favour.

RESOLUTION TO A GENERAL MEETING

IF YOU DECIDE to put a resolution to a General Meeting you should:

> ✔ **Call a general meeting in accordance with your constitution**
>
> ✔ *Give members written notice of the resolution*
>
> ✔ **Take steps to ensure that as many members as possible attend the meeting**
>
> ✔ *Record the number of members attending the meeting*
>
> ✔ **Take a vote of all members**
>
> ✔ *Take a vote of all tenants (including leaseholders) who are members*
>
> ✔ **Take a vote of secure tenants who are members**

DOOR-TO-DOOR SURVEY

To carry out a door to door survey you need to:

● **Give each member a copy of the proposal in writing**

● **Carry out a survey which records:**

- Members' names
- Whether secure tenants,

leaseholders or other types of resident
- Whether the person votes *'yes' - 'no' or 'don't know'*

BALLOT

IF THE BALLOT option is chosen, members should be given written notice of the proposal and the ballot arrangements should be clearly explained.

Each member should be given a ballot form. Giving secure tenants and leaseholders different coloured forms will help you to ensure that you can count these separately as well as part of the total.

The ballot boxes can be placed in well-used locations or taken door-to-door to ensure a high turnout.

I Said Ballot, Not Ballet!

SERVING A RIGHT TO MANAGE NOTICE

THE VOTE, survey or ballot must show that a majority of all tenant (including leaseholder) members who voted, including a majority of secure tenants who voted, are in favour of the organisation exercising the Right to Manage.

Positive vote

If there is a positive vote in favour, the next step is for the Chairperson and Secretary of the organisation to serve a notice on the local authority. An example notice is included in *Appendix 2*.

You must make sure you deliver a copy of the notice to each house which will be affected by it. The local authority must reply within one month. If the council does not accept your notice, it must tell you why in writing.

GETTING COUNCIL ASSISTANCE

ONCE THE proposal notice is accepted, you can ask the council for training, office accommodation and other facilities which you think are necessary.

You are unlikely to need an office straight away. That probably won't be needed until just before you start managing the estate.

The council must reply to written requests for assistance within two months of each request. Most councils will be happy to meet reasonable requests and to provide other support and assistance.

However, if you are not satisfied with the support offered or if the council is unwilling to help, you can go to an arbitrator. This is an independent person who tries to settle disputes.

Arbitration

The arbitration procedure is described briefly below and the full procedure is set out in the *Modular Management Agreement for Tenant Management Organisations.*

New Barracks, Salford

ARBITRATION

SETTING UP a tenant management organisation is a long and complex procedure.

It is unlikely to be plain sailing all the way and there may be times when you, the agency and the local authority disagree over important points.

Negotiation

In most cases, it should be possible to resolve differences through negotiation. However, where problems and disputes arise at key points and cannot be overcome, the TMO or the council can seek arbitration.

These key points are:

The *Chartered Institute of Arbitrators* have set up an Arbitration Procedure and the Secretary of State has approved a panel of arbitrators.

Costs

This is not a free service. The *Chartered Institute of Arbitrators* have a registration fee. There is a fixed charge for a simple arbitration - where both sides send documents and papers for a decision.

If the problem is more complex, or if the parties want to state their case at a hearing, the costs will be higher.

Binding

The outcome of the arbitration is binding on both parties and the arbitrator can award costs. This means that if the arbitrator agrees with the council or the agency, your group may have to pay costs.

Because there is a cost involved, every attempt should be made to resolve differences informally. But the formal arbitration procedure is a safety net as a last resort.

Norley Hall, Wigan

CHAPTER 3
Feasibility Studies & Development Programmes

INTRODUCTION

ONCE YOU HAVE served your *Right to Manage* notice, and had it accepted by your local authority, you can start looking at the possibilities for increasing tenant involvement in your area in more detail.

The first stage of this process is to carry out a feasibility study. This includes a programme of support and training which will help you to look at the options for managing your estate.

If the feasibility study shows that a TMO is feasible and there is a vote in favour of a TMO by a majority of tenants, a TMO development programme begins.

Training

The development programme is intended to provide you with the training that is necessary for you to manage the estate when your TMO is fully operational.

It includes the practical work necessary to get the TMO off the ground, such as developing its legal constitution and negotiating the terms of the management agreement with the council according to the Modular Management Agreement.

In the Right to Manage Regulations, feasibility studies are called *'initial feasibility studies'* and development programmes are called *'full feasibility studies'*.

However, the terms feasibility study and development programme are the ones most commonly used.

The feasibility study and the development programme must be carried out by a training agency on the Department of the Environment's Approved List *(see Chapter 5 and Appendices 4 and 5 for more on this).*

Agency help

The agency will help you through the feasibility study and development programmes, and arrange the training you need.

At the feasibility stage, the agency is responsible to the Department of the Environment for the work programme. But at the development stage the responsibility for applying for funding and running the programme is yours.

Looking at plans, Newark & Sherwood

Framework

At both stages the main activities of the programmes must be based on a common framework published by the Department of the Environment in *Preparing to Manage*.

This gives a fuller account of the content of feasibility studies and development programmes, of the proportion of time to be devoted to each kind of activity, and presentation of work programmes.

More information on training can be found in *Learning to Manage*.

FEASIBILITY STUDIES

OBJECTIVES

THE MAIN OBJECTIVE of the feasibility study is to explore whether it is possible to increase the involvement of tenants in the management of their estate. It looks particularly at the possibility of setting up a TMO.

The feasibility study does this by helping you to explore the options for running your estate in the future from just being more involved in decisions right through to taking on ownership of the estate.

Control

It also informs all tenants (not just the committee) about the possibility of extending tenant control, and involves them in the decision about whether to go further through a ballot or poll.

The feasibility study is likely to last up to six months. On a small estate, with an experienced group of tenant activists, the timescale could be reduced. On a large estate, with a relatively inexperienced tenants' group, it might take a bit longer.

KEY ELEMENTS OF THE FEASIBILITY STUDY

THE MAIN ELEMENTS of a feasibility study are summarised in the checklist below.

All feasibility studies must contain these elements, although there can be flexibility in the order of some of them in the programme, and the number of hours spent by your agency.

The detailed content of feasibility study work programmes must always be tailored to the needs of your estate.

Checklist -
Key Elements of the Feasibility Study

- **Planning the study**
- *Assessing the estate's problems and priorities*
- **Assessing the demand for tenant involvement**
- *Exploring management options*
- **Understanding housing management and finance**
- *Preparing for a management role*
- **Assessing competence**
- *The feasibility report*
- **The 'test of opinion'**
- *Planning for the development stage*
- **Communication**
- *Monitoring*

- **Find out what feasibility studies are designed to cover**
- *Identify your own training needs*
- **Discuss and agree the work programme**
- *Agree on the committee's role and responsibilities during the feasibility stage*
- **Liaise with the local authority**
- *Inform tenants of the start of the study*

PLANNING THE STUDY

This is always the first activity of a feasibility study. Working with your agency you should:

Throughout the study you should hold regular meetings with your agency and the council to monitor progress.

ASSESSING THE ESTATE'S PROBLEMS & PRIORITIES

THIS IS USUALLY the single largest activity for the agency during feasibility. The estate assessment should usually cover:

- **Housing conditions**
- *Housing management*
- **The estate's physical environment (open space, roads, etc)**
- *Amenities (shops, services etc)*
- **Social and economic conditions (unemployment, types of household)**

Assessing dampness, Angell Town

This assessment should also consider the problems experienced by people living on the estate, and how increasing tenant control could help solve them.

The assessment will usually be carried out by a combination of:

- **Collecting information and reports from the local authority**

- *Talking with residents, through surveys or discussion groups*

- **Interviews with council officers and other agencies working on the estate**

ASSESSING THE DEMAND FOR TENANT INVOLVEMENT

THE FEASIBILITY STUDY
must promote the understanding of tenant involvement among tenants in the area. Keeping residents in the area informed is absolutely vital.

Working with your agency, you need to try and get as many people involved as possible. You can do this through:

- ✔ **Door-to-door surveys**
- ✔ **Exhibitions**
- ✔ **Open days**
- ✔ **Public meetings**
- ✔ **Newsletters**

EXPLORING MANAGEMENT OPTIONS

You need to consider whether a TMO is right for your estate, or whether other options would be better. This element of the feasibility stage involves learning about:

- **Options which stop short of full tenant management, such as estate sub-committees**

- *TMOs, and what they can offer*

- **Transferred ownership options, such as transfer to a housing association**

UNDERSTANDING HOUSING MANAGEMENT

YOU WILL NEED to find out how the council works, and how it delivers its housing management service.

This is essential for you to see what a TMO could do, and how it fits in with the council's responsibilities.

PREPARING FOR A MANAGEMENT ROLE

THIS PART OF the feasibility study is also training for the TMO committee. It covers the skills and approach needed to lead the community.

Training will typically include:

- **Working as a group**
- **Representing the community**
- **Leadership and negotiation skills**
- **Equal opportunities**

ASSESSING COMPETENCE

THE AGENCY'S ROLE includes monitoring your group's progress towards competence as a potential management committee of a TMO.

If the agency does not think that you will become competent, the feasibility study can be brought to an early close.

There is some information on what the agency will be assessing at the end of this chapter. You can find out more about competence in *Preparing to Manage.*

THE FEASIBILITY REPORT

IT IS THE AGENCY'S job to produce a written feasibility report, after discussing the draft with you. This report is sent to the Department of the Environment and the local authority.

The feasibility report explains the feasibility study and gives an assessment of the estate and the abilities of the tenants' committee. It concludes whether or not a TMO is a desirable and achievable objective for you.

If the agency concludes that it would be beneficial to set up a TMO on your estate, the next step is to organise a *'test of opinion'* among tenants in the area.

THE 'TEST OF OPINION'

IF THE FEASIBILITY report concludes that it would be helpful for your area to set up a TMO, the ultimate assessment of demand for resident involvement at the feasibility stage is the *'test of opinion'.*

All tenants (including leaseholders) in the area should have the chance to express their views. The agency's job is to notify all the tenants in the area and carry out a ballot or poll.

PLANNING FOR THE DEVELOPMENT STAGE

IF A MAJORITY of those voting say *'yes'* in the ballot, (including a majority of secure tenants), you can proceed to the development stage. This must start within six months of completing the feasibility study.

Some planning for this next stage should take place at the end of the feasibility programme by:

- **Finding out more about development programmes**

- ***Appointing an agency for the development stage***

- **Identifying your training needs**

- ***Developing ideas about the content of the development programme***

- **Liaising with the local authority**

COMMUNICATION AND MONITORING

COMMUNICATION with tenants and other agencies and monitoring progress, are both vital activities. You need to hold regular meetings with people who will be affected by the programme.

DEVELOPMENT PROGRAMMES

OBJECTIVES

THE DEVELOPMENT stage is intended to bring you to the point when you can be a fully-functioning TMO, in charge of an agreed range of management functions on your estate.

The development programme helps you to achieve this by providing essential training in the skills and knowledge necessary to run a TMO.

Negotiate

You will also negotiate a management agreement with the local authority, defining responsibilities and rights. The development programme is likely to last up to about two years.

KEY ELEMENTS OF THE DEVELOPMENT PROGRAMME

THE MAIN elements of the development programme appear in *Preparing to Manage.* These are summarised in the following checklist.

All development studies must contain these elements, but there is flexibility in the order of some of them in the programme, and the proportion of time spent by your agency on each.

The content of your development programme must reflect the needs of your group and your estate.

Checklist – Key elements of the Development Programme

- **Planning the programme**
- *Agreeing the TMO group's role and responsibilities*
- **Becoming 'Incorporated'**
- *Introducing the Modular Management Agreement*
- **Working up the management options**
- *Preparing to run a TMO*
- **Negotiating the management agreement**
- *Assessing competence*
- **The development report**
- *Assessing tenants' support*
- **Setting up the TMO**
- *Communication*
- **Monitoring**

PLANNING THE PROGRAMME

TOGETHER WITH your chosen agency, and with the local authority, you must agree and plan the programme before any other work starts. This usually means:

- **Finding out more about development programmes**
- *Identifying your own training needs*
- **Discussing a draft work programme and finalising the programme**
- *Liaising with the local authority, and agreeing council input to the programme*
- **Informing tenants about the development programme**

Throughout the development stage, you should hold regular meetings with your agency and the local authority to review progress.

AGREEING THE TMO GROUP'S ROLE & RESPONSIBILITIES

AS A GROUP, you need to anticipate the management responsibilities you will take on when the TMO eventually goes live.

This part of the programme ensures that you decide how your group is to be organised during the development stage. *It will include:*

- **Training on options for management structures**

- *Deciding on sub-committees, committee and officer roles*

- **Deciding on who is responsible for what, and who can make decisions**

BECOMING 'INCORPORATED'

THERE IS A LEGAL requirement to 'incorporate' the TMO as an Industrial and Provident Society, or as a company limited by guarantee, or as a company limited by shares, before you can enter into a management agreement with the local authority. Your agency can help you to arrange this at the appropriate time.

INTRODUCING THE MODULAR MANAGEMENT AGREEMENT

THE MODULAR Management Agreement sets out the choices that can be made about which management functions your TMO will take over from the council.

It also offers choices about the level of your responsibility. This part of the programme will include:

- **Training for your committee on the Modular Management Agreement**

- *Training on how the Modular Management Agreement could be applied on your estate*

WORKING UP THE MANAGEMENT OPTIONS

YOUR TMO WILL be looking to take over a range of functions from the local authority.

This part of the development programme is designed to help you decide exactly which functions you want to take responsibility for and how much responsibility you want to take.

Training

Making these decisions involves quite detailed training on managing functions like rent collection, housing allocations, housing repairs and caretaking. What you cover in the training will depend on the functions you want to take over.

After training, you will need to take decisions on the parts of the Modular Management Agreement that you want to apply. You will also need to decide what policies and practices your TMO will operate for each of the functions you take over.

This part of the development programme is likely to take several months to get through.

PREPARING TO RUN A TMO

AS A TMO, you will be responsible for a sizeable budget, and for managing any staff you employ directly.

A TMO is a medium-sized business operation and you need to have the skills and knowledge to run it. The group will need to learn how to do this effectively.

In this part of the programme, together with your agency, you should:

- **Consider staffing options for the TMO**

- *Examine how to recruit and employ staff*

- **Learn about business management skills such as financial budgeting, performance review, the use of computers, and the management of contracts**

NEGOTIATING THE AGREEMENT

CONCLUDING THE management agreement with the local authority is likely to need extensive negotiation to arrive at a position which suits both parties.

The development programme covers:

- **Training in negotiating skills for the TMO**

- *Negotiating with the local authority about the Management Agreement*

- **Negotiating with the local authority about start up arrangements, management and maintenance allowances and office premises**

At the end of this stage you will have a full set of proposals about how the TMO will be set up and how it will work in practice.

ASSESSING COMPETENCE

AS AT THE feasibility stage, your agency will assess whether your group is competent to take over housing management responsibilities.

If the agency does not feel that your group is likely to progress towards full tenant management it will submit an early report, setting out the reasons for bringing the programme to an end.

Arbitration

The local authority, as the owner of the properties, will also be very interested in your group's abilities. The council has a right to challenge the agency's view and seek arbitration if it does not feel that you are ready to take over the responsibilities.

THE DEVELOPMENT PROGRAMME REPORT

TOWARDS THE END of your development programme your agency must prepare a report on the development of your TMO. *This report should:*

- **Describe the development process**

- *Set out the proposed terms of the management agreement for your TMO*

- **Assess your TMO's competence to carry out each of the tasks it proposes to take on**

- *Make recommendations to the Department of the Environment about whether or not your TMO should proceed*

ASSESSING TENANT SUPPORT

Following a satisfactory development programme report, your agency must publicise the proposal to set up the TMO to every tenant.

Agreement

The publicity must give a summary of the proposed management agreement, and a full copy of the agreement must be available for inspection by tenants.

The agency will then set up a ballot asking whether or not tenants support the proposal for a TMO. A good turn out is essential.

The ballot must be secret and can be conducted door-to-door, by post, or by using a polling station. A majority of all the tenants in your TMO's area must vote in favour.

SETTING UP THE TMO

IF A MAJORITY of those eligible to vote approve the TMO, you must sign the management agreement with the council within three months.

During the handover period there are a range of other tasks necessary to set up the TMO, such as:

- **Finalising your TMO's management structure**
- *Setting up and equipping the office*
- **Recruiting staff**
- *Establishing systems of record-keeping and administration*

- **Arranging for the handover of functions from the council**
- *Launching your TMO*

There is a detailed checklist in *Appendix 3* which will help you to make sure that you have all your systems in place.

COMMUNICATION

AS AT THE FEASIBILITY stage, it is vital that you ensure that you have good communication with local residents.

The TMO is a collectively-controlled organisation and, for success, needs tenants to support it.

You can continue to encourage involvement by holding meetings and open days, carrying out surveys and producing newsletters.

MONITORING

THROUGHOUT the development stage, you should hold regular meetings with your agency and the local authority to review progress. The Department of the Environment will also need regular progress reports.

COMPETENCE TO MANAGE

IT IS IMPORTANT that all agencies apply the same standards to their view of competence.

To ensure this, the DoE has drawn up a list of things which tenants must be able to do, and systems which must be in place at the end of the feasibility and development stages.

These are available in *Preparing to Manage.*

WHAT IS COMPETENCE?

SAYING THAT someone is competent is saying that they can do a job in a capable manner.

So assessing competence is measuring someone's ability to do something, not their knowledge of how to do it.

This may sound like a problem because you cannot show that you are able to run a TMO until you have done it.

Tasks

However, as the previous sections have outlined, there are lots of tasks which your group will need to do during the feasibility and development stages.

These can be used to show that you are competent to manage.

HOW IS COMPETENCE ASSESSED?

The TMO competences look at three things:

- **Whether individual members of the TMO have the skills and abilities needed**

- *Whether the group, as a whole, has the range of abilities needed*

- **Whether systems and procedures, which the TMO must have, are in place**

There are no tests or exams involved in looking at whether people can do a task.

Competence is assessed by looking at what people do, talking to them, and asking other people who have seen them carrying out tasks.

The tasks which are assessed are those which committee members do in the course of setting up a TMO.

Programme

Your committee will be fully involved in drawing up the work programme and deciding what you need to learn. The agency will help you to make sure that you have covered the areas you need to be competent in.

By the end of the development programme, you will have set up all the systems and policies that the TMO will need.

The last part of the TMO competences assessment simply checks that these are in place.

WHAT DO THE TMO COMPETENCES COVER?

THE COMPETENCES you will need will depend on which functions the TMO will manage.

For example, if you are taking over repairs, you will need to show that you can develop repairs policies, systems and procedures. You will do this as part of the development programme.

There are a number of competences which all TMOs need. These include:

> ✔ **Ability to work in a team**
>
> ✔ *Ability to assess options*
>
> ✔ **Ability to exercise financial control**
>
> ✔ *Ability to develop policies and procedures*
>
> ✔ **Ability to manage the organisation**

You will be able to build on previous experiences, learn how to do these, and gain practice throughout the feasibility and development programmes.

DOES EVERYONE NEED TO BE COMPETENT?

THERE ARE SOME abilities which all your committee will be expected to have by the end of your programme, for example, working as a team member.

For other tasks, such as planning and controlling budgets, only a few people need to be competent.

Both the agency and the local authority will want to ensure that all the competences are covered - but these can be spread across different committee members.

DO THE TMO COMPETENCES LEAD TO A QUALIFICATION?

THE TMO competences themselves are not qualifications, but many are based on *National Vocational Qualifications* (NVQs). These are work-place qualifications which are recognised by employers.

Gaining TMO competences may help you to gain NVQs, if you wish. Your agency will be able to tell you more about this.

FUNDING

SECTION 16 FUNDING

MOST FUNDING to develop tenant management comes from the Department of the Environment which has a grant scheme administered by the Tenant Participation Branch. The grants are called *Section 16 grants.*

The grant is intended to cover the costs of agreed work programmes. The amount which can be claimed depends on the number of council homes in your area. (The DoE will give you details of current maximum allowances).

FUNDING FOR AGENCIES

AGENCIES AGREE what their hourly charge will be with the Tenant Participation Branch at the beginning of each financial year.

This hourly rate must be used by the agency for all its promotion and feasibility work.

Surprise

Tenants' groups are often surprised at the cost of agency workers' time (between £25 and £45 per hour) and think that employing someone direct will be cheaper.

You must remember though, that the person you appoint must be approved by the Department of the Environment and must have suitable experience.

The agency will ensure that the people working with you are competent. Their charge also covers the provision of offices, equipment and administration.

Budget

At the development stage, many agencies have to charge VAT on top of their hourly rate. You need to take this into account in your budget.

Agencies on the Department of the Environment's Approved List *(see Appendix 5)* claim Section 16 grant direct for the promotion and feasibility stages.

At the development stage, tenants claim the grant themselves. This is to ensure that the TMO becomes responsible for managing a budget.

You can pay the agency to administer the grant for you, but you have overall responsibility for it.

CLAIMING THE GRANT

TO RECEIVE the grant at the development stage, you need to make an application for funding. This will set out your planned work programme and costs.

Once the grant has been approved by the DoE, you claim the grant each quarter.

Expenses

Before the claim can be made, you will need details of all the hours that have been spent on the previous quarter and the cost, as well as any expenses which are to be claimed.

It is very important that you begin the grant claims process well in advance of the deadline, to allow time to collect the information.

WHAT THE GRANT CAN BE SPENT ON

YOU MUST appoint an approved agency to oversee your development programme, but you can decide how much you want the agency to do *(see Chapter 5).*

Some groups use some of the money to employ an administrator. This is particularly useful if your area is very large.

Advice

The money can also be used to pay for specialist advice and training on areas like employment law, contracts and computer training.

You may also have expenses for creche facilities, translation costs and travel costs for study visits and attending conferences and seminars.

The grant may also be used to buy office equipment, provided that this has been approved by the DoE.

LOCAL AUTHORITY CONTRIBUTION

ONCE YOU HAVE exercised the *Right to Manage,* you can ask the council for training, office accommodation and other facilities which you think are necessary.

You must make sure that your requests are reasonable for your stage of development.

Initially, it would be reasonable to ask for support and training to help you appoint an agency and for access to rooms for meetings and training.

Equipment

Later on, when you are getting ready to take over management, you could reasonably ask for an office and office equipment. If the council is unwilling to help you can go to an arbitrator *(see Chapter 2).*

The local authority must also make a 25 per cent contribution to your development grant. The DoE pays the other 75 per cent.

You should set up a payment arrangement with the council because if it is paid late you may have cash flow problems.

SPENDING WISELY

YOUR DEVELOPMENT grant could add up to quite a lot of money (depending on the size of your estate). You must make sure that you spend it wisely and get value for money.

An important part of your development programme is about learning how to control your budget - a new skill for many tenants' groups.

Essential

Financial control is an ability that you will find essential when you take over responsibility for managing your area. The skills and knowledge that you develop will be essential in the long term.

PEP have produced a book called *'Managing the Money'* which may help you to look after your development grant.

CHAPTER 4
Modular Management Agreement

INTRODUCTION

THE GOAL YOU are aiming for in setting up your TMO is to take on some of the jobs the council does in managing your homes.

You may only want to take on one or two things that most concern you, like getting small repairs done or the stairs cleaned.

Alternatively, you may want to take on most of the jobs the council does because you think you can provide a better service.

Council's agent

In taking on the jobs you want to do to improve the management of your homes, your TMO is acting as the council's agent.

What your TMO does is to act on the council's behalf in doing the jobs you decide to take on. The council remains the legal landlord and you remain tenants of the council.

Agreement

Whether you take on a few jobs or a whole range of management tasks you will need a management agreement between your TMO and the council.

The council owns the property in which you live. You cannot manage it, even when you exercise the Right to Manage, unless you enter into a management agreement with the council.

WHAT IS A MANAGEMENT AGREEMENT?

THE MANAGEMENT agreement is a legal document which does four things:

- **It says what jobs your TMO is going to do and what jobs the council is going to continue doing**

- *It sets out the way you are going to do the jobs you take on (your policies and procedures)*

- **It sets out the standards you should achieve in carrying out the jobs you take on, (your TMO's performance standards)**

- *It sets out the standards the council should achieve in carrying out the jobs it is going to carry on doing, (the council's performance standards)*

The management agreement is a very important document. It contains the practical details of how your TMO is to use the Right to Manage to manage your homes.

It is the agreement between you and your council under which the council delegates to your TMO the power to do the jobs you want to do on its behalf.

In managing your homes, your TMO only has the power to do what the management agreement says you can do.

THE MODULAR MANAGEMENT AGREEMENT

YOU WOULD FIND the Right to Manage very difficult to exercise if, once you decided what jobs you wanted to take on, you had to negotiate a management agreement with your council from scratch.

Model agreement

To make it easier for tenants who want to exercise the Right to Manage, and for councils in permitting tenants to exercise that right, the Department of the Environment has published a model management agreement.

Tenants will want to take on different jobs. Tenants on one estate may want to collect rents and deal with rent arrears. On another estate, they may not want to have anything to do with rent collection or arrears.

For this reason, the model management agreement has different options from which you can choose the level of management responsibility you want to take on.

Because it has different options (or 'modules') the management agreement is called a 'modular agreement'. To make reference to it easier in this Chapter, the Model Modular Management Agreement is called *'the Model Agreement'*.

From the various model clauses, you can choose which option gives you the level of responsibility you want to take on.

Pick & choose

The idea is that you pick and choose the options you want and, like a jig-saw, build up a management agreement which sets out the involvement you want in managing your homes.

One thing you cannot do is to change the wording of the optional clauses in the Model Agreement.

The reason for this is that the Model Agreement sets out the jobs the Government thinks tenants ought to be able to take on if they want to manage their homes.

Cross references

You must also not change the numbering of clauses, even if you choose to omit a clause which is optional.

The reason for this is that there are cross references to other clauses and other chapters in the Model Agreement. These cross references will not make sense if you change the clause numbering.

THE STRUCTURE OF THE MODULAR MANAGEMENT AGREEMENT

TO MAKE IT EASIER to read and understand, the Modular Management Agreement is divided into eight chapters. These are as follows:

1. **Principles of the Agreement**
2. **Repairs and Maintenance**
3. **Rent and Service Charges**
4. **Financial Management**
5. **Tenancy Management**
6. **Staffing and Management of Relationship with the council**
7. **Monitoring and Performance Standards**
8. **Definition of Terms**

MODEL AGREEMENT CLAUSES

EACH CHAPTER is divided into clauses. Each clause deals either with an aspect of your TMO's dealings with the council or one of the many management jobs which need to be done.

The clauses dealing with management jobs contain the modular options. **Option A** is always the lowest level of responsibility. This usually leaves the job with the council, but with the council having an obligation to consult your TMO and tell you what the council is doing.

As you move up the options to **option B, C, D** etc the level of responsibility you take on increases.

The highest level options generally give your TMO full responsibility for a particular job, with the council left simply monitoring your performance from the information your TMO is required to give the council.

'Defined terms'

In some of the clauses in each chapter you will find what are called *'defined terms'*.

These are where some concept or reference which appears more than once is given a short label to avoid lengthy repetition. For example the Right to Manage Regulations is shortened to *'The Regulations'*.

All these defined terms appear in **Bold Letters** wherever they are found in the Model Agreement. For easy reference, all these defined terms are listed in *Chapter 8* of the Model Agreement.

'Variable terms'

There are also what are called 'Variable Terms' which appear in **BOLD CAPITAL LETTERS** in the Model Agreement.

These are things which will vary from one TMO to another - that's why they are called *variable terms*. For example the address of the TMO's registered office will vary.

To make it easy to build up your management agreement, all these variable terms are collected together in clause 1 of *Chapter 8* of the Model Agreement.

This makes is easy for you to fill in all the *variable terms* needed to make your agreement specific to the management of your homes. You don't have to search through the clauses for spaces to fill in.

PRINCIPLES USED IN DRAFTING THE MODULAR MANAGEMENT AGREEMENT

THE MODEL AGREEMENT

may look a formidable legal document when you first look at it. *Don't let that put you off.*

It was written by a team of people who have a lot of experience helping tenants manage their homes. It contains the best practice learned from the experience of tenants who have managed their own homes.

In writing the Model Agreement the team aimed to apply the following principles:

✔ **To provide a fair and balanced agreement between the TMO and the council**

✔ *To offer a range of options which can be mixed and matched to meet what tenants want and to suit local needs*

✔ **To give some flexibility in the management policies and procedures adopted, to provide for local practice and procedures to be used**

✔ *To avoid legal jargon and write in clear and simple sentences*

✔ **To maintain a sensible structure so that relevant issues appear together**

34

- ✔ **To build in performance standards and performance monitoring**

- ✔ **To build in commitment by the TMO to equal opportunity practice, procedures and monitoring**

- ✔ **To enable TMOs to increase or decrease their levels of management responsibility**

- ✔ **To ensure that existing experience of successful tenant management arrangements are built in**

HOW TO USE THE MODEL AGREEMENT

DON'T START BY reading the whole Model Agreement. You will find it long and probably boring and, probably, confusing.

Start by looking at the tables at the beginning of the Model Agreement. These summarise the clauses and options in each chapter and explain what effect they have.

With the help of your agency, discuss these options with other tenants involved in developing the Right to Manage proposals for your housing.

Building up

Once you have an idea of what you want to do, start looking at the clauses and options in each chapter.

Begin building up the management agreement which meets your needs by

choosing the clauses which most closely reflect the jobs and levels of responsibility you want to take on.

Once you have firmed up your ideas, you can produce a draft of your management agreement by selecting the model clauses you have chosen.

Computer disk

The Model Agreement is available on computer disk, so you don't even have to type out your choices.

Once you have chosen your clauses from the options available your agency can print out a draft of the management agreement you want to use.

CHOOSING WHAT YOU WANT TO DO

SUBJECT TO YOUR TMO meeting the required minimum level of competence for each task, the Model Agreement makes it possible for you to mix and match the level of responsibility you take on for different jobs.

This allows you to build up your own management agreement from the modular clauses so that your management agreement precisely fits the jobs you want to do and the level of responsibility you want to take on.

Agency help

Your agency will help you decide which jobs you want to take on and which option in each clause reflects the level of responsibility you wish to have in doing that job.

35

One of the things the Model Agreement doesn't do is allow you to take on the supervision of contracts let by the council. This reflects government policy that there should be a separation of duties between the council and the TMO.

This doesn't stop the council and the TMO having a separate contract which allows the TMO to supervise council contracts. It just isn't part of the Model Agreement.

DECIDING HOW YOU ARE GOING TO DO THE JOBS YOU TAKE ON

DECIDING WHAT you are going to do is the easier bit. Deciding how you are going to do it and setting the standards you need to achieve to do the job well is more difficult. This is where you will need the help and guidance of your agency.

Repairs Committee, Langridge Crescent

To complete the preparation of your management agreement you will need to prepare the appendices to be included at the end of each chapter. These set out:

- **The way you are going to do things**

  and in respect of key jobs,

- **The performance standards you are going to aim to achieve in doing the job**

The Model Agreement does not include sample appendices you must use. The way you carry out key jobs and the standards you aim to achieve is for you to decide, in consultation with your council.

Local practice

The content of the appendices to be included in your management agreement will reflect existing local practice, your wishes and the wishes of your council.

Your agency will also be able to advise you on the best practice to include in your appendices.

Practice guide

You will also find a guide called *The Housing Management Standards Manual* published by the Institute of Housing to be a useful source of good practice guidance and advice. (This guide costs £350, so you may want to look at it at your local Library!)

To help you and your agency draft your appendices the Model Agreement contains checklists of items which the team who drafted the agreement think ought to be included.

These are intended as a guide only, but if you ensure that the appendices written for your management agreement cover all the items in the checklist, your council will be less likely to challenge the policies and procedures you propose.

EQUAL OPPORTUNITIES

YOUR EQUAL OPPORTUN-ITIES Policy and Procedure, which must be included as an appendix to *Chapter 1*, is very important.

Your management agreement must contain a firm commitment that your TMO will implement equal opportunities and fair housing practices.

Koran Class, Samuda, Isle of Dogs

Monitoring

You must also monitor your performance and provide performance information regularly to show that you are behaving fairly and without discrimination in every aspect of your work in managing your homes.

Checklist - Equal Opportunities

Your Equal Opportunities Policy and Procedure must include:

● **A list of the laws you must comply with**

● *The aims and objectives of your equal opportunities policy*

● **How you are going to achieve your equal opportunities objectives**

● *How you are going to ensure that you operate fair allocations policies if you are involved in letting*

● **How you are going to ensure that you operate equal opportunity practices in employing staff and contractors**

● *Details of how you are going to monitor your equal opportunities performance in carrying out the various jobs you take on*

Experience of tenant control shows that tenants who want to discriminate are a small minority.

Most tenants, probably because they have seen or experienced first-hand the unjust effects of discrimination, are keen to operate fair policies and procedures.

You have a moral and legal duty to ensure that your TMO does not discriminate against any person in carrying out the tasks you take on under the management agreement.

NEGOTIATING YOUR MANAGEMENT AGREEMENT WITH YOUR COUNCIL

ALTHOUGH YOU have the Right to Manage your own homes it will still be necessary to negotiate your management agreement with the council.

The best way to exercise your Right to Manage is with the active consent of your council.

Full support

You are going to have to work with them to ensure the smooth running of your homes, so it is better to have the council's full support for what you are taking on, how you are going to do the job and the performance standards you aim to achieve.

Begin your discussions early with the support of your trainer or agency. Ask the council to comment on what you propose and for help in drawing up the appendices which will set out your working practices, policies, procedures and standards.

In this way you and the council can make sure that what you aim to do fits in with the council's established policies and practices.

Digmoor Neighbourhood Office, West Lancashire

Foundation

This will lay the foundation for easier working relationships between your TMO and the council in the years to come.

Easy co-operative working relationships save everyone a great deal of time and money, so it is important to get things started off on the right foot.

If your council doesn't co-operate or refuses to negotiate your management agreement, you have the right, under the Right to Manage Regulations, to go to arbitration to get your management agreement approved.

Minimum levels

The arbitrator will want to know that you meet the required minimum levels of competences and that your proposed appendices to the management agreement meet the requirements set out in the checklists in the Model Agreement (or, if they don't, that there is a good practical reason for them not doing so).

Arbitration should be the last option. An agreement negotiated with your council is best.

GETTING PAID FOR THE JOBS YOU TAKE ON

YOUR TMO MUST be paid for taking on the job of managing your homes. If you take on repairs, you will need to pay your own repairs team or other contractors to carry out those repairs.

You may need to employ staff to carry out management tasks such as collecting rents, dealing with arrears and inspecting properties at the end of tenancies.

'Allowances'

In the Model Agreement, what you get paid are called *'Allowances'*. Your agency will help you to work these out by using the method set out in the booklet *Calculating Allowances for TMOs.*

This method helps you to work out what you get paid by looking at the jobs you take on and the costs the council would incur in doing those jobs (less a small amount, called an efficiency saving, because your TMO will not have the central overhead costs a council has to carry).

Agency help

The method is a detailed financial calculation. You will certainly need the help of your agency to work out the allowances you should be paid for the work you are taking on.

If your TMO intends to manage a large number of homes and take on a high level of responsibility, you will probably need the help of a financial consultant to agree your allowances with the council.

It is important that the allowances calculation is right so that you have enough money to do the jobs you are taking on.

CHAPTER 5
Selecting An Agency

INTRODUCTION

AS CHAPTER 2 explained, the Right to Manage procedure is triggered when your tenants' organisation serves a notice on your local authority.

When the council accepts the proposal notice, you will need to appoint an approved agency to provide you with support and training.

Study

The agency will carry out a feasibility study. If the feasibility study is completed successfully, you need to appoint (or re-appoint) an agency who will have the responsibility of taking your group through the development stage.

It is very important that the agency appointed at both stages is the right one for your group.

This chapter takes you through the process of appointing an agency to help you make the right choice. It covers:

- **The roles of agencies, local authority and DoE**
- **Selecting an agency**
- **Making a choice**
- **Value for money**

The research carried out by the University of Glasgow/TPAS (Scotland) found that the best combination of support was a partnership between the tenants, an independent agency and council staff.

Other people, with specialist knowledge, might be drawn in at particular stages. The roles of the council, agencies and the Department of the Environment are detailed in *Appendix 4* but an outline is given below.

ROLE OF AGENCY

AGENCIES CAN help you to develop a TMO in a number of ways. However, there are some jobs which all approved agencies must be able to do, as a condition of their funding. A checklist of these key tasks is given below.

Checklist
- Role of Agency

- **Help you work out what you need to know**
- *Set up a work programme*
- **Assess whether your organisation is competent**
- *Write a report at the end of feasibility and development*

- **Help you to make choices and negotiate a management agreement**
- *Organise a ballot or poll*

OTHER HELP & ADVICE

Apart from the jobs which an agency must carry out, they can also help you by:

✔ **Acting as an *'honest broker'* in your negotiations**

✔ **Helping with information and consultation campaigns**

✔ **Monitoring progress and making sure that you are heading in the right direction**

ROLE OF THE LOCAL AUTHORITY

LOCAL AUTHORITIES have a responsibility to assist tenants' groups to develop a TMO under the Right to Manage.

Many councils do this willingly because they support tenant management. The Right to Manage Regulations say that local authorities must provide reasonable support.

Some councils have a specialist section who deal with TMOs. If not, a senior member of staff will usually be given responsibility for working with you.

The role of the local authority is outlined in the following checklist.

Checklist - Role of Local Authority

- **Give information and training to tenants' groups**
- *Support development of TMOs*
- **Check that your tenants' organisation has a valid constitution**
- *Provide reasonable resources*
- **Work in partnership with you and the agency**
- *Provide information and training*
- **Negotiate a Management Agreement**
- *Decide whether to challenge the agency's reports*
- **Provide allowances for management and maintenance**
- *Monitor the performance of established TMOs*
- **Provide ongoing support**

Information and training

ROLE OF THE DEPARTMENT OF THE ENVIRONMENT

THE DEPARTMENT of the Environment's Tenant Participation Branch deals with many aspects of the development and training of TMOs.

The role of the branch is outlined in the checklist below.

Checklist - Role of Department of the Environment

● **Promote tenant participation and tenant management**

● *Administer the Section 16 grant scheme*

● **Approve agencies for work with TMOs**

● *Monitor the quality of training provided*

● **Ensure value for money**

● *Check the Management Agreement*

● **Support research and publications**

WHICH AGENCIES ARE APPROVED BY THE DOE?

AS A RESULT of the growth of tenant management there are now a number of agencies willing to carry out training and development work with TMOs.

All agencies who work with TMOs must be approved by the Department of the Environment. The DoE look at the skills and knowledge of these agencies, their ability to do the job and their cost.

Criteria

The checklist or criteria used by the DoE in considering whether or not to approve agencies is provided in *Appendix 5.* You can get the list of approved agencies direct from the DoE.

If you have a specific agency or trainer in mind who is not on the list you can approach them. They may be able to get approval to support and train you. *Appendix 5* also gives information on how to apply for approval.

WHO TO APPROACH

THERE WILL BE a number of agencies who are able to provide support to your group. You will have to choose one agency to do the job.

You should collect information from a number of sources about agencies, to find out what they can do and their previous experience.

42

GENERAL PUBLICITY

MOST AGENCIES produce publicity and information about the service they offer.

Start by contacting the agencies who work in your area and requesting this information. They may be willing to let you have a copy of the report they wrote to get DoE approval.

PERSONAL EXPERIENCE

IF MEMBERS of your group are already active in tenants' associations, they may have attended events organised by some of the agencies.

Ask what they thought of the training provided. But remember, carrying out feasibility studies for a prospective TMO may require different skills and experience to organising a one-off training event.

TAKE ADVICE

TALK TO HOUSING staff, especially specialist tenant participation workers. They may have worked with particular agencies or know something of their reputation.

The Department of the Environment can give you names and addresses of other TMOs who may also be able to provide advice.

WHY LOOK AT A NUMBER OF AGENCIES?

YOU MAY FEEL you already know which agency you want to work with. You may be already working with an agency, or the council may have recommended a particular agency.

But how will you know whether this agency can provide the support best suited to your needs if you don't *'shop around'?*

Tenders

Many tenants' organisations choose to put the job of providing support and training *'out to tender'.* This involves asking a number of agencies to tell you what they can provide and how much it will cost.

You can consider as many agencies as you wish but it is usually helpful to limit the number invited to tender for the job. Between 3 and 5 is usually about right.

Best agency

However you go about it, choosing an agency with staff who are competent and with whom you get on well will not be easy.

Getting the best agency for the job depends on how clear you are about what you want the agency to do and what skills and experience you are looking for.

You need to draw up your own *'shopping list'* and prepare carefully for making this important decision.

Checklist - Steps Involved in Choosing an Agency

- **Decide who will be involved in choosing the agency**

- *Get training for those involved in appointing the agency*

- **Draw up a brief for the job - set out what you want the agency to do**

- *Decide what you are looking for and shortlist applicants*

- **Carry out interviews**

- *Make a decision*

MAKING A CHOICE

WHO SHOULD BE INVOLVED?

IT MAKES SENSE for the same people from your group to be involved in all of the steps in choosing an agency.

However, the selection process is best carried out by a small, though representative, sub-committee.

It is important that their decision is supported by everyone, so it is a good idea for membership of the sub-committee, its tasks and report-back arrangements to be discussed and agreed at a full committee meeting.

Support

The council may want one of their staff to give you support and advice, including being present at the interviews. Local community workers involved with your group may also be able to help.

Checklist - Appointing a Sub-Group

- **Discuss and agree membership**

- *Agree tasks and responsibilities of group*

- **Agree timetable for making a decision**

- *Receive regular reports on progress*

TRAINING FOR THE SELECTION GROUP

CHOOSING THE right agency needs careful planning and preparation. The people involved need interviewing skills and knowledge of good practice in recruitment, including equal opportunity issues.

Your council may be able to help you to obtain training to select an agency at the feasibility stage. Your feasibility programme should include training for selecting a development agent.

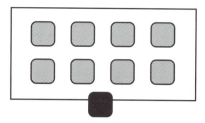

recruitment

DRAWING UP A BRIEF FOR THE JOB

A BRIEF IS an outline of the tasks that you want an agency to carry out. This does not need to be a long and complicated document but there are some things that you should include.

First, the Brief needs to include general information which will give agencies a picture of the background to your group and why you want to explore the idea of setting up a TMO.

Second, you need to decide what you want an agency to do. This may depend on the help which you can get from the council. Agencies can offer a variety of services *(see Appendix 4).* Think carefully about the kind of support that you need from them.

Function range

If you already know what sort of TMO you want to set up and the range of housing management functions you want to take over then this should also go in the Brief. However, if you are not sure say so - and ask that the agency covers all the options and possibilities.

The Brief should be sent to agencies which you would like to consider, to help them prepare for an interview with you.

Details

In addition to asking agencies to tell you how they would carry out the job described in the Brief, you should ask for details about their background, experience and costs.

A checklist of the things you should cover in the Brief is given below and an Example Brief is included in *Appendix 6.*

Checklist - Brief for a Training Agency

- **Aims and objectives of the group - what do you hope to achieve?**

- *History of the group*
  - *Members' skills and experience*
  - *Level of community support*

- **Stage in development**
  - Promotion
  - Feasibility
  - Development

- *Description of your estate, the housing and tenants*

- **What support is available from the council and elsewhere**

- *Details of the job to be done (see role of agency and Appendix 4)*

- **Timetable for completing the job**

- **Ask for:**
  - Background and work of the agency
  - Qualifications and experience of staff
  - Number of hours work involved in carrying out the tasks
  - Details of costs per hour
  - References from previous clients

SHORTLISTING APPLICANTS

WHEN YOU HAVE received responses to your Brief, the next step is to shortlist the applicants. This involves looking at whether:

> ✔ **The agency can do the job**
>
> ✔ *The staff have the right skills and knowledge*
>
> ✔ **The proposals offer value for money**

It is usually helpful to limit the shortlist to no more than three agencies

CAN THE AGENCY DO THE JOB?

LOOK BACK to the Brief and what you are asking the agency to do. From the information you have about the agency, its experience, the staff and current workload, will it be able to do the job?

If you have no experience of working with a particular agency you will have to try and answer this question using the information you have been sent.

Checklist - Can the Agency do the Job?

● **Has the agency worked with other TMOs?**

● *Have you got references?*

● **How long has the agency been established - has it a track record?**

● *How experienced are its trainers?*

● **How many other groups is the agency working with - does it have enough staff?**

OK, can we have the 'Miss Personality' test now please?

DO AGENCY STAFF HAVE THE SKILLS AND KNOWLEDGE?

THE DOE WILL have checked that the agency has some experienced staff but you need to check that the people who would be working with you have the right skills and knowledge.

Ideally, you should aim to work with one or two people employed by an agency, to provide continuity throughout the development of your TMO.

However, it is unlikely that any one person will have all the necessary skills and experience you need. So you may need to look for an agency which can provide a number of staff with different backgrounds.

Ask questions

Alternatively you will have to work out where the gaps are and ask questions to find out whether they can be filled by using specialists or council staff.

It will help if you write down the skills, knowledge and experience you are looking for - your *'shopping list'*. Look for a combination of:

> ✔ **Practical experience of developing TMOs**
>
> ✔ *Knowledge of housing management repairs and finance*
>
> ✔ **Understanding of local authorities**
>
> ✔ *An ability to communicate / negotiate*
>
> ✔ **Training skills**
>
> ✔ *Accountability to clients*

An example 'person' specification is given in *Appendix 7*.

Which particular skills, knowledge and experience are most important to your group will depend on what you need to learn to achieve the aims and objectives in your Brief.

The following questions may help you decide what you are looking for:

Checklist - What Do You Need Help With?

● **Does the group need help to become an effective team?**

● *Do you need training in committee and meeting skills?*

● **Will you need help to negotiate the management agreement?**

● *Will you need people with financial skills to negotiate the allowance?*

● **Are council staff able to carry out training in policies and procedures?**

● *Will a council tenant participation worker be available to give advice to the group?*

● **Are the majority of tenants supportive of a TMO or are you struggling to keep people involved?**

● *Is your group representative of everyone who lives on the estate?*

PRIORITISING

YOUR SHOPPING LIST will probably end up a long one. You will need to decide which items are essential and which only desirable.

There may also be some special requirements, for example being able to work in the evenings and weekends, which are relevant.

EQUAL OPPORTUNITIES

BE CAREFUL THAT all the requirements you have listed are directly related to training your group for the task of running a TMO.

Will you be able to assess easily whether the requirements are met during an interview? This is important to prevent discrimination and bias creeping in.

Shopping list

Your shopping list of experience and skills will allow you to compare different agencies in a fair and effective way.

It will make it more difficult for disputes to arise during the interview process and reassure those not directly involved that your decision is a good one.

INTERVIEWING YOUR CHOSEN AGENCIES

INTERVIEWS ARE about getting more information from the agencies about their ability to work with you. Good preparation and planning is essential.

You will need to work out in detail where and when the interviews will take place, who will act as Chairperson and whether you want someone on hand to welcome people.

Informal chat

It is a good idea to give agencies the opportunity to have a look round the estate and chat informally about the group and its plans. You could also ask the agency to make a presentation to the interview panel.

This would let you see their style of working. Once you have decided these aspects you can write to the agencies telling them what to expect.

Questions

Next, you need to draw up a list of questions and decide who will ask them. Try to share out tasks during the interview so everyone has a chance to ask questions and listen to the answers.

It is useful to use a form to record how well each agency meets your requirements.

Checklist - The Interview

- **Introduce the interview panel**
- *Allow time for a presentation*
- **Ask specific questions**
- *Allow the agency to ask questions*
- **Check who will be working with the group on a day-to-day basis**
- *Discuss issues such as start dates, payment, hours involved*
- **Inform the agency when the decision will be made**

48

MAKING YOUR DECISION

ONCE THE INTERVIEWS are completed you will need to choose one agency to work with you. Hopefully, it will be clear from your checklists which agency seems best placed to provide you with the support and training you need.

If you are not sure which agency to choose, try to reach agreement by going back over your notes about:

> ✔ **How well the agency can carry out your Brief**
>
> ✔ **How closely their staff match your shopping list of skills and experience**

If you still can't reach agreement consider holding a second interview.

VALUE FOR MONEY

IN ADDITION TO considering whether the agency is suitable and how closely their staff match your shopping list of skills and experience, you will also need to consider whether the work to be done represents value for money.

WHAT IS VALUE FOR MONEY?

ASSESSING VALUE for money is not just about comparing prices to see who offers the most hours for the least money. Good value for money means looking at the *quality* of what's on offer as well as the *quantity*.

This means that you should assess costs after you have looked at how well the agencies can do the job set out in the Brief and the skills and knowledge of their staff.

HOW DO YOU ASSESS VALUE FOR MONEY?

THERE ARE guidelines laid down by the Department of the Environment about maximum costs for developing TMOs. You will need to make sure that the costs of your chosen agency are within the guidelines.

The Department will not approve grants which are above the recommended limits.

Compare

However, you should go further than this. You need to compare the quantity and quality of the service on offer with the price being charged.

You will need to ask all the agencies tendering to provide details of their costs in a way that will allow you to make comparisons between them.

Breakdown

You should ask the agencies to provide a breakdown of the likely cost of their work programme in terms of the number of hours of staff time involved in:

- ✔ **Administration e.g. completing forms, writing reports**

- ✔ **Travel time (if the agency is based some distance away this may be high)**

- ✔ **Preparation time for meetings or training events**

- ✔ **'Contact' time e.g. attendance at meetings or training**

- ✔ **Costs of the ballot**

You should also check whether costs are included for such things as:

- ✔ **Study visits**
- ✔ **Specialist trainers**
- ✔ **Producing information for residents**
- ✔ **Training materials**
- ✔ **Training equipment**

When you compare the details of different agencies costs you may find you are being offered very different numbers of hours spent in direct contact with your group.

Time Spent

Some agencies may be spending much more time on administration and preparation. Others may be charging separately for some costs covered in the hourly rate of other agencies.

If there are big differences between the agencies who tender for the work, you will need to look closely at their proposals and try to work out:

- ● **What is causing these differences?**

- ● **How will it affect the advice, support and training your group should receive?**

Checklist - Making a Decision

- ● **How far can the agency match your Brief?**

- ● *How well do the agency's staff match your shopping list of skills and experience?*

- ● **Is price a consideration?**

- ● *Resolve any differences of opinion*

- ● **Interview again if two agencies seem equally able to do the job**

CHAPTER 6
Working With An Agency

INTRODUCTION

THE PREVIOUS chapter covered choosing the right agency to work with you. Equally important is setting out the 'ground rules' for how you and the agency will work together. There are three main tasks involved in this:

✔ **Drawing up an agreement**

✔ *Monitoring the agreement*

✔ **Raising problems and settling disputes**

DRAWING UP AN AGREEMENT

THE PURPOSE OF an agreement is to ensure your chosen agency does what it said it would do in its written proposal and at the interview.

If you did your homework to produce a clear Brief *(see Chapter 5)* it should be fairly straightforward to draw up an agreement.

The agreement will also set out what assistance and payment the agency should get in return for doing the job.

Responsibilities

The agreement gives both your group and the agency certain responsibilities and rights. The council may be able to provide you with advice and guidance in drawing up the agreement to ensure it is fair to everyone involved.

WHAT THE AGREEMENT SHOULD COVER

THE TERMS and conditions set out in the agreement will depend on your particular circumstances and the job to be done. However, it should cover the following areas.

Checklist
- Agreement with Agency

● **Objectives - the job to be done**

● *Tasks involved*

● **How well the tasks should be done**

● *Staff and their roles*

● **Number of hours involved**

● *Costs and who is responsible for payment*

● **Overall responsibility for completing the contract**

● *Review of progress*

● **Whether and how changes can be made**

● *Handling complaints and disputes*

MONITORING THE AGREEMENT

ONCE YOU HAVE an agreement drawn up you need to ensure that everyone sticks to it. Both parties have to meet their side of the bargain.

It is best if you set down on paper how the agreement will be monitored. A summary of how this is to be done should be in the agreement itself.

The arrangements must be practical and supported by everyone involved. Monitoring arrangements usually involve:

✔ **Regular meetings**
✔ **Occasional reviews of progress**
✔ **Raising problems and settling disputes**

REGULAR MEETINGS

THE WORK involved in developing a TMO is complicated. Getting the work done needs a certain amount of organisation and co-ordination of effort.

This can be done in regular meetings between your group and the agency. You may also need to involve the council in some, or all, of these meetings.

Decisions taken at meetings need to be minuted or confirmed in writing.

OCCASIONAL REVIEW MEETINGS

IN ADDITION TO the regular 'business' meetings you will need to take time to stop and review overall progress towards your aims and objectives.

These sessions will require some preparation and perhaps more time than the regular sessions. Most groups have such reviews every 3-6 months.

The objectives of review meetings should be to:

✔ **Ensure the work programme is being carried out satisfactorily**
✔ **Identify any changes necessary**
✔ **Discuss any problems and work out how to resolve them**

RAISING PROBLEMS AND SETTLING DISPUTES

YOU WILL BE working with your agency for many months on complex and difficult issues. It would be surprising if your group did not experience some problems and set-backs along the way.

How well your agency is able to carry out the work programme may be affected by circumstances beyond their control.

Difficulties

If you have worked out in advance how to tackle difficulties and settle differences between you, the relationship should be much smoother.

You will need to discuss this issue with your agency and with the council who have an interest in your progress. Here are some suggestions:

- **Agree that problems should be raised as they arise and solutions sought there and then**

- *If difficulties remain they can be discussed at your next regular meeting*

- **Nominate certain members of the group (e.g. Office Bearers) to handle serious problems in between meetings**

- *Identify an independent third party who could provide advice if the problem cannot be resolved*

ARBITRATION

THE RIGHT TO MANAGE procedures provide for certain serious disputes to be referred to arbitration, if efforts at conciliation fail.

G STAFF

over responsibility for managing your estate, the job that the committee or board has been preparing for really begins.

In the handover period you will have appointed staff, set up your office systems and sorted out liaison with the local authority.

Now you have the opportunity to put your skills and knowledge into practice. The most important things that the committee needs to do are:

> - **Manage the TMO staff**
> - **Monitor the performance of the TMO**
> - **Provide information to the local authority**
> - **Keep in touch with residents**

You may also wish to think about branching into other activities or taking on additional management responsibilities. This chapter looks at each of these issues in turn.

You have the choice, when setting up your TMO, between:

> - **Employing staff to carry out the day-to-day tasks**
> - **Contracting services from an agency**
> - **Doing the jobs yourselves**

Some TMOs will have a mix of all three.

Most TMOs, except the very smallest, have staff to carry out at least some of the day-to-day tasks involved in running a TMO. The number of staff will depend on the size of the organisation and the responsibilities it takes on.

A small TMO (up to 100 properties) may only need one worker while a large TMO (over 1000) homes could have 10 to 15 workers or more.

Partnership

It is vitally important that the TMO committee or board works in partnership with employees.

The success or failure of the TMO may depend on how well you work together. Being a good employer is an important part of this.

Being a good employer means making sure that you are offering a reasonable salary for the amount of responsibility involved and good conditions of employment.

However, this does not mean that you should accept poor conduct or performance. You need written job descriptions, contracts of employment and grievance and disciplinary procedures.

STAFF SUB-COMMITTEE

IF YOU ARE employing staff, it is likely that you will have established a staffing sub-committee during the development stage.

The members of the committee should also have received training on employment issues such as:

✔ **Equal opportunities in employment**

✔ *Recruitment and selection*

✔ **Committee / staff roles**

✔ *Staff supervision*

✔ **Contracts of employment**

✔ *Dealing with discipline and grievances*

✔ **Staff welfare**

✔ *Staff appraisal*

You will also find it helpful to have someone to go to for advice if you have problems. This could be a personnel officer in the local authority, a legal advice centre or a solicitor who specialises in employment law.

The *Employment Handbook* (CATCH, 1993) covers a lot of these issues and is a recommended buy for your library.

STAFF SUPERVISION

YOU NEED someone on the committee (probably the Chair) to be responsible for day-to-day supervision and support for employees.

It is often helpful to have a regular, weekly meeting with the most senior member of staff to discuss work priorities and problems.

Easier

This is much easier than having someone who reports to a dozen bosses or trying to manage by dropping in and interrupting work in progress.

You may find it useful to draw up a structured staff appraisal scheme in which standards of performance and targets are set.

STAFF TRAINING

TMO WORKERS can often be isolated and find it difficult to keep up to date. Even if you don't have much money, it is important that you find ways of making sure that staff have opportunities to attend seminars and meet other TMO workers.

The book, *Learning to Manage* has more information on this.

MONITORING PERFORMANCE

ONE OF YOUR main reasons for setting up a TMO is likely to have been to provide a high standard of housing management and repairs services to tenants in the area.

You need to make sure that you are doing this by getting regular reports on the service, and financial statements at committee meetings. Your management agreement will have set out the areas that you need to monitor *(see Chapter 4).*

Information

What information you need will depend on which jobs you have taken on. The most important things that you need to check are equal opportunities, whether services are meeting targets and financial information.

The following checklist gives some examples.

Checklist - Monitoring Performance

✔ **Equal opportunities monitoring for employment**

✔ *Number and type of enquiries to the office*

✔ **Number of empty properties and length of time empty**

✔ *Reasons for properties lying empty*

✔ **How much rent has been lost due to empty houses**

✔ *Information about the waiting list for houses*

✔ **Information about who has been housed**

✔ *Number of repairs reported*

✔ **Number of repairs outstanding (beyond target dates set)**

✔ *How much has been spent on repairs*

✔ **What rent is owed**

✔ *Action taken for people with rent arrears*

✔ **Number of tenancy disputes and action taken**

✔ *Information on cases of racial or other harassment*

✔ **How much money has been spent - and on what**

✔ *Information on whether you are spending more or less than you expected*

Acknowledgement to H. Chandler (1991) 'The Right Information' PEP.

Getting regular information (monthly, quarterly and annually) will help you to see where problems might be arising and take action.

You should also get information about how the council is performing the jobs it is still responsible for.

MONITORING BY THE LOCAL AUTHORITY

YOUR LOCAL AUTHORITY will also want to know about your performance and will want to be sure that the TMO is managing effectively.

Arrangements for monitoring will have been set out in your management agreement *(see Chapter 4).*

Standards

Every year the council will assess the performance of the TMO and will agree a series of *'performance standards'* with you.

These standards are likely to be for things like equal opportunities; level of arrears; speed of repairs; length of time that properties are empty; and financial control.

They should be similar to standards set for local authority management and maintenance in areas like yours.

COMPARING AREAS

THIS MEANS THAT you need to agree which area, or areas, your TMO should be compared with. It is important you make sure that, as far as possible, the council is comparing like with like.

If your properties are unmodernised, and many of the tenants in your area are unemployed, then you should not be compared with an area where properties are in good condition and where most people are in work.

'Comparators'

It is likely that you will have collected a lot of information about your area during the feasibility and development stages.

You can use this to check that the *'comparator'* area is similar to yours. The key things that you could try to match are given in the checklist below.

Checklist - Comparing Performance with Another Area

- **Is the area similar to the TMO area?**
- *Has the area got about the same number of properties?*
- **Are the houses the same age?**
- *Are they the same type?*
- **Are they in the same condition?**
- *Are the types of household (families, elderly, single people) similar?*
- **Is the proportion of tenants on Housing Benefit about the same?**

It is unlikely that you will get an exact match on all of these but make sure that the comparison is one that you are happy with.

If there is no area which is similar, make sure that differences are taken into account when performance is compared.

FINANCIAL COSTS

THE ANNUAL discussions will also include negotiations on the management and maintenance allowances which the TMO will receive the following year.

The way this is worked out will be contained in the management agreement (see Chapter 4).

Running Costs

As part of the assessment of costs, the council may compare the costs of running the TMO with the costs of managing the comparator area.

If the costs of running the TMO are a lot higher than the costs of managing a similar area, the council can end the management agreement.

REASONS FOR ENDING THE AGREEMENT

IN ADDITION TO the costs of running the TMO, the council will want to be satisfied that the TMO is keeping its finances in order and that your rules, procedures and standing orders are being followed.

If the council finds evidence of malpractice or serious inefficiency, then the management agreement can be terminated.

RELATIONS WITH THE COUNCIL

IN PRACTICE, most TMOs have a satisfactory working relationship with the council. Many local authorities are very supportive and will offer advice and assistance.

If you have a good partnership it is worth working to keep it that way - divorce can be hard on both sides.

KEEPING IN TOUCH WITH RESIDENTS

THE MOST IMPORTANT people to assess the success of the TMO are the residents of the area.

While the TMO was being developed, you will have worked with your agent and put a lot of time and effort into making sure that tenants were kept informed and had a chance to participate.

Participation

It is important that you keep up the level of participation. Make sure that you keep in touch with what residents think and take their views into account.

Assessing tenant satisfaction

Even though the constitution ensures that the TMO is democratic, accountable and representative there is a danger that committee members will lose touch.

Residents' Views

If your area is small, committee members will probably have a good idea of what residents think of the TMO.

But you should not take this for granted. The views below are from residents in two small TMOs. Which would you prefer to be?

> 'They are quite willing to listen and if there is anything you want to say, you just say it.'
>
> Resident - TMO 'A'

> 'They are a clique, a secret society. No-one knows what's going on... If you need a repair it comes down to the personality.'
>
> Resident - TMO 'B'

TENANT PARTICIPATION POLICY

ONE WAY THAT you can make sure that you keep in touch with residents is to have a tenant participation policy. This could involve all, or some, of the things on the checklist.

Checklist - Participation

✔ **All information in plain English**

✔ *Translation of essential information*

✔ **Information available on tape or in braille**

✔ *Regular newsletter produced*

✔ **TMO handbook produced**

✔ *People encouraged to join the committee / board*

✔ **Opportunities for training offered to residents**

✔ *Open committee meetings*

✔ **Committee is representative of people in the area**

✔ *Co-option is used to make sure minority groups are represented (if necessary)*

✔ **Support given for social activities to improve the community**

✔ *Satisfaction surveys carried out*

✔ **Complaints procedure set up**

✔ *Attendance at general meetings and AGM encouraged*

✔ **Tenants encouraged to become members**

OTHER ACTIVITIES

MANY PEOPLE think that tenant management organisations are not just there to provide a good housing service, but that they should also provide a service to the community.

TMOs may offer assistance to other groups in the area by providing rooms for meetings, access to machinery (computers, photocopiers, typewriters) and small financial donations to community groups.

Activities

In some cases people who have been involved in TMOs have gone on to become involved in other community activities or to set up other organisations with complementary aims.

Examples include TMOs which have been the starting point for:

- **Employment training initiatives**

- **Playgroups**

- **Youth centres**

- **Community businesses**

- **Credit unions**

You may want to assess whether the TMO is providing wider social benefits to the area.

This sort of evaluation would be useful if the TMO was seeking funding from other sources to develop other community activities. It might also be used to prove the benefits of having a TMO to the local council.

KEEPING A RECORD

IF YOUR GROUP wanted to assess the wider benefits of the TMO, the simplest way would be to keep a record of local activities the TMO had been involved in.

Contributions could be financial - such as small donations to community groups; made in kind - such as help with printing and photocopying or allowing a room to be used for meetings.

Assistance

Assistance could also be given by TMO committee or board members or by staff helping out at local events.

AN INDEPENDENT STUDY

IF YOU ARE seriously seeking large grants for community activities then a more detailed study, carried out by outside consultants, might be appropriate.

This would usually involve interviews with people involved in the TMO and local professional workers. It might also include a survey.

CHANGING YOUR MANAGEMENT RESPONSIBILITIES

THE DECISIONS you take about the jobs you take over from the council are not rigidly fixed. If you want to start cautiously and see how you manage with a few key jobs before taking on more responsibility you can do that.

The Modular Management Agreement has a standard clause which allows you to increase (or decrease) the jobs you take on and the level of responsibility you have.

Any time you want to increase your responsibilities your TMO must:

> ● **Show that you have competence to carry out any new job or increased responsibility you want to take on,**

and,

> ● **Pass a resolution at a general meeting to vary your management agreement,**

and,

> ● **Give the council three months written notice that you wish to change your management agreement**

You have the right to change your management agreement. Like any right, it should be exercised responsibly.

Changing your management agreement involves you and your council in a great deal of work. Make sure that it is a positive, controlled and planned expansion of your role in managing your own homes.

Continuity

Remember that the effect of frequent changes can only be a poorer service for you and other tenants because continuity in day-to-day management and decision making is important.

If you don't want to take on everything you want to do on day 1, the Modular Management Agreement has a clause which allows you to take over responsibility for different jobs on different starting dates.

Discuss the practicalities of this with your agency and with the council.

New Barracks, Salford

Appendix 1

A MODEL CONSTITUTION FOR TENANT MANAGEMENT ORGANISATIONS

NAME AND AREA

1. The NAME of the organisation is _____

2. The DEFINED AREA in respect of which the organisation may serve a proposal notice under the Housing *(Right to Manage Regulations 1994)* is the area shown in the map attached.

3. This defined area is within one local authority area *(name of local authority)*.

AIMS

4. The AIMS of the organisation are to:

   4.1 Promote membership to all people eligible to join the organisation

   4.2 Promote equal opportunities within the community

   4.3 Improve the housing and other services in the area of the organisation

   4.4 Be non-party political

   4.5 Promote social, welfare, recreational and training activities for the benefit of members of the organisation

   4.6 Represent the majority view of the members

   4.7 Build a partnership and improve communication between landlord and membership

cntd.

4.8 Provide regular information to all members

4.9 Regularly consult all members

4.10 Monitor the organisation, its work, finances and membership

4.11 Provide and promote training for members on areas
of the organisation's activity and concern.

EQUAL OPPORTUNITIES

Either:

5. THIS ORGANISATION shall positively promote equal opportunities
within the community and within its membership, work for the
elimination of discrimination against persons on the basis of
race, gender, age, sexuality, disability and religion.

Or:

5. THIS ORGANISATION shall uphold equal opportunities and
work for good relations among all members of the community,
specifically prohibiting any conduct which discriminates or
harasses on the grounds of race, gender, age, sexuality,
disability and religion.

Or:

5. THE ORGANISATION, in all conduct of its affairs, prohibits
discrimination or harassment on grounds of race, gender,
age, sexuality, disability and religion.

MEMBERSHIP

6. MEMBERSHIP of the organisation shall be open to all secure
tenants or other tenants of dwelling-houses of the local
authority in the defined area.

7. A RECORD of all members in the current year shall be kept
by the Secretary of the organisation.

8. Any MEMBERSHIP FEE shall be determined by the
Annual General Meeting.

ASSOCIATE MEMBERSHIP

9. The COMMITTEE may accept any person as an Associate Member. They shall have all the privileges of membership except the right to vote at meetings and to be elected as members of the committee.

10. The SECRETARY shall keep a record of all members.

ENDING MEMBERSHIP

11. MEMBERSHIP shall end when a member ceases to be a local authority tenant in the defined area, dies, or resigns.

12. In the event of GROSS MISCONDUCT membership can be suspended or ended by a two-thirds majority vote of the committee.

13. A MEMBER whose membership has been suspended in accordance with *clause 12* shall be entitled to have that suspension reviewed at the next general meeting of the organisation.

MEETINGS

The Annual General Meeting

14. The ORGANISATION shall hold an Annual General Meeting (AGM) once in each calendar year, and not more than 15 months shall pass between the date of one AGM and the next.

15. The AGM shall:

    - Receive an annual report from the committee
    - Present audited accounts to members
    - Appoint an independent auditor
    - Elect the committee
    - Consider any resolutions put forward by members
    - Vote on any amendments to the constitution.

16. All MEMBERS shall be given 21 days written notice of the AGM, and this must include an agenda, minutes of the last AGM, details of nominations to the committee and any resolutions which include any proposed changes to the constitution.

cntd.

17. Any PROPOSED CHANGES to the constitution or nominations to the committee must be notified and sent to the Secretary in writing at least 28 days before the AGM.

GENERAL MEETINGS

18. Each year the organisation shall hold at least three GENERAL MEETINGS (including the AGM) which shall be open to the general membership.

19. All MEMBERS of the organisation shall receive 14 day's notice of General Meetings.

20. The GENERAL MEETINGS shall be minuted.

21. The QUORUM for all general meetings shall be 10 members or 5 per cent of the membership, whichever is the most.

SPECIAL GENERAL MEETINGS

22. A SPECIAL GENERAL MEETING may be called by the Committee and must be called by the committee if requested by at least 10 members or 10 per cent of the membership, whichever is the most, at least 28 days before the date on which those members request the meeting to be held. The Secretary must send to each member written notice of a Special General Meeting 21 days in advance of the meeting.

VOTING

23. Each member shall have ONE VOTE on any resolution put before an AGM, General Meeting or Special General Meeting.

24. All VOTING that takes place at an AGM, General Meeting, Special General Meeting and Committee Meetings, shall be counted and recorded in the minutes.

25. If there is a tie the Chair will have an extra casting vote.

MINUTES

26. All VOTING that takes place at an Annual General Meeting, General Meeting, Special General Meeting and Committee Meetings, shall be counted and recorded in the minute.

27. All FORMAL MEETINGS such as Committee Meetings, Special General Meetings and Annual General Meetings must be minuted and the minute formally approved by the next meeting of the Committee or General Meeting respectively.

28. All MINUTES shall be available for inspection by members of the organisation.

THE COMMITTEE

29. Any MEMBER over the age of 18 shall be entitled to stand for election to the committee

30. The COMMITTEE shall stand down at each Annual General Meeting and may be re-elected.

31. There shall be at least six COMMITTEE MEMBERS and at least 50 per cent shall be tenants.

32. There shall be at least 5 COMMITTEE MEETINGS each year.

33. All MEMBERS shall be given not less than seven days notice of each Committee Meeting, at which any member shall be entitled to attend (but not to vote).

34. The OFFICERS of the committee shall all be tenants.

35. The COMMITTEE may from time to time as necessary create any sub-committees and / or working parties on a permanent or temporary basis. The members of any such sub-committee or working party shall be selected by the committee from among its members. Any such sub-committees or working parties shall report to the committee for decision making.

36. The committee shall MONITOR the work, finances and membership of the organisation.

cntd.

37. The committee shall REPORT to each General Meeting on the work done by the committee since the last General Meeting.

38. The committee shall PRODUCE Standing Orders which it may revise from time to time to govern the conduct of Committee Meetings.

OFFICERS OF THE COMMITTEE

39. The ORGANISATION shall have a Chairperson, Secretary and Treasurer.

40. The CHAIRPERSON shall chair the General and Committee Meetings. The duties of the officers shall be defined in the standing orders of the organisation.

41. The OFFICERS shall report to each Committee Meeting and General Meeting of their work.

42. There shall be no more than two committee MEMBERS from the same household.

CO-OPTEES

43. The COMMITTEE may co-opt non-voting members onto the committee in order to fill vacancies that occur during the year or to ensure appropriate representation of all people in the community.

FINANCE

44. The TREASURER shall open a bank or building society account in the name of the organisation and keep records of the organisation's income and expenditure. The treasurer shall report the balance in the account to the committee at each Committee Meeting.

45. The COMMITTEE shall appoint three authorised signatories for any cheques and cheques shall be signed by at least two of the authorised signatories. The signatories should be from different households and not related to one another.

cntd.

46. The ORGANISATION'S ACCOUNTS shall be kept up to date and annual accounts for each year shall be independently audited and shall be presented to the Annual General Meeting.

47. The ACCOUNTS of the organisation shall be available for inspection by any member of the organisation who requires to see them, within 28 days. The request for inspection must be made in writing to the Treasurer.

48. The TREASURER is authorised to pay from petty cash travel and other expenses to representatives of the organisation undertaking the organisation's work providing that each payment is supported by a receipt, ticket or voucher. Each such payment of petty cash shall be signed by the receiver. The Treasurer shall provide a list of petty cash payments to the committee, at each Committee Meeting.

INFORMATION

49. The ORGANISATION shall provide information to all members on things that affect the organisation and its members.

50. Every MEMBER of the organisation shall be given a copy of the constitution when they join. Members shall be given copies of any changes to the constitution.

51. MINUTES of all General Meetings and Committee Meetings shall be available from the Secretary for all members.

DISSOLUTION OF THE ORGANISATION

52. The ORGANISATION can only be dissolved by a Special General Meeting called specifically to consider a motion to dissolve the organisation.

53. All MEMBERS shall be given 21 days written notice of such a meeting, which shall contain the wording of the resolution.

54. The ORGANISATION shall only be dissolved if two-thirds of members present at the Special General Meeting vote for a motion to dissolve the organisation.

55. The SPECIAL GENERAL MEETING shall decide on disposal of assets, funds and equipment.

Appendix 2

EXAMPLE
RIGHT TO MANAGE PROPOSAL NOTICE

TO THE DIRECTOR OF HOUSING *(or equivalent officer):*

Date

This letter gives notice that, in accordance with regulation 2(1) of the Housing (Right to Manage) Regulations 1994, *[name of your organisation]* wishes to exercise the Right to Manage in relation to the following housing and land in its area: *[identify housing and land, perhaps by a map]*

Our constitution meets the conditions in regulation 1(4): I attach a copy. A copy of this notice has been delivered to all the dwellings to which it refers.

We have the necessary membership of the tenants of the housing to which this notice relates:.

- *total number of tenants (including leaseholders) in the identified housing:*

- *total number of tenants (including leaseholders) in the identified housing who are members of [name of your organisation]:*

- *total number of secure tenants in the identified housing:*

- *total number of secure tenants (including leaseholders) in the identified housing who are members of [name of your organisation]:*

A vote of members was taken on this proposal on *[dates(s)]*, with the following results:

cntd.

- *total number of tenants (including leaseholders) in the identified housing who are members of [name of your organisation] and who voted:*

- *total number of secure tenants in the identified housing who are members of [name of your organisation] and who voted:*

- *total number of tenants (including leaseholders) in the identified housing who are members of [name of your organisation] and who voted in favour of the Right to Manage proposal:*

- *total number of secure tenants in the identified housing who are members of [name of your organisation] and who voted in favour of the Right to Manage proposal:*

[Signed]

CHAIRPERSON   **SECRETARY**

Appendix 3

Checklist -
Handover of Responsibilities

DURING THE development of the TMO, the Management Agreement becomes a crucial document. Once the Management Agreement is approved and signed, and the final ballot has taken place, the TMO will have a handover period.

This checklist provides a guide to the policies, systems and procedures which should be set up during the handover period. It will help you to ensure that your TMO is ready for business when you take over responsibility for managing the area.

COMPANY REQUIREMENTS / RECORDS

THE TMO MUST KEEP company records on file to comply with rules and legislation.

- a) Has the TMO got a signed and agreed Management Agreement, complete with appendices?

- b) Has the TMO registered as an Industrial and Provident Society or a Company limited by guarantee or by shares?

- c) Is there an up to date membership / share register?

- d) Has the TMO got adequate and up-to-date insurance cover?

POLICY FILE

The TMO should maintain a file of its policies and procedures which should be kept up to date. It should contain the policies which will be described in the Management Agreement. It will vary from TMO to TMO depending on functions undertake but may include:

cntd.

1) Equal opportunities Policy and Procedure

2) Maintenance Policy and Procedure

3) Financial Procedures

4) Rent Arrears Policy and Procedure

5) Allocation Policy and Procedure (including transfer / exchange)

6) Tenancy Agreement

7) Tenant Complaints Procedure

8) Duties of Office Bearers (Chair, Treasurer, Secretary)

9) Terms of Reference for Sub-committees

10) Training Policy and Procedure

11) Tenant Participation Policy and Procedure

OFFICE SYSTEMS

THE OFFICE SYSTEMS required will vary considerably between TMOs, depending on size and the jobs taken on.

A TENANCY RULES

1) Has each property / tenancy got its own tenancy file?

2) Is there a signed tenancy agreement on file?

3) Is there information on file on Housing Benefit.

4) Are tenancy files kept in a secure place?

5) Are equal opportunities monitoring procedures established?

B RENT and ARREARS

1) Is there an adequate rent collection system which offers a choice in payment methods?

2) Will the rent accounting system keep weekly rent records for each tenant showing rent due, rent paid, balance of credits / arrears carried forward, arrears action?

3) Does the system provide rent account information for management purposes?

cntd.

4) Is the system established to comply with the rent arrears procedure?

5) Has the TMO had its paying-in books printed?

6) Has the TMO established systems for rent information with bank / post office

7) Are standard arrears letters established?

8) Are standard Notices Seeking Possession prepared?

9) Has the TMO established adequate void control procedures?

C MAINTENANCE FILES

MANY TMOs WILL OPERATE a computerised maintenance system. Manual systems may operate in conjunction and include plans, work specifications, previous maintenance records and details of equipment in the property.

1) Is there a system for TMO tenants to report repairs that need doing?

2) Will the system record all repairs reported?

3) Has the policy established target timescales for repairs?

4) Is there a list of approved building contractors in place?

5) Is there a system for maintaining estimates for work?

6) Is there a system for checking a percentage of repairs when works are complete?

7) Will there be adequate cover for out of hours or emergency repairs?

8) Will the system allow for committed repairs expenditure to be measured against budget?

9) Are there copies of service agreements on file (for example, gas, boilers, lifts, entry phones)?

10) Has the TMO established a procedure for planned preventative maintenance and cyclical maintenance

11) Will the system allow the TMO to produce annual reports to tenants and require reports to the LA?

12) Will the system produce adequate information to ensure overall management control of the maintenance system?

cntd.

D   CARETAKING AND CLEANING

1) Have the TMO established cleaning rotas for caretaking and agreed standards

2) Has the TMO established the equipment and cleansing material requirements of caretakers

3) Has the TMO established the arrangements for grounds / garden maintenance

E   FINANCE

1) Are adequate and up to date records kept of invoices paid, payment advice notes, cheque stubs, bank statements, cash book and bank reconciliations?

2) Are payments authorised and cheques signed according to procedure laid down?

3) Are there regular reports on financial matters to the TMO committee and General Meetings?

4) Has the TMO established its budget?

5) Has the TMO established a cash flow forecast?

6) Is the TMO registered for VAT?

7) Are audited accounts available for inspection?

8) Is there a set of banking procedures for handling money received?

9) Has the TMO set up an adequate petty cash system?

10) Are bank accounts established in line with Management Agreement?

11) Is the TMO satisfied it will be able to meets its management obligations from allowances?

F   EMPLOYMENT

1) Are there copies of job descriptions and person specifications for each employee?

2) Is there a contract of employment for staff?

3) Are arrangements in hand for employment of staff?

cntd.

4) If employed, are offer letter and acceptance letter on file?

5) Are references for each employee on file?

6) Is there a policy and procedure in place for staff training?

7) Is the TMO prepared for dealing with PAYE and National Insurance?

8) Has the TMO established a procedure for ethnic and gender monitoring of applicants / staff?

G   TENANT PARTICIPATION AND SUPPORT

1) Are public meetings / general meetings held regularly?

2) Are most residents members of the TMO

3) Are regular newsletters produced?

4) Was there a good turnout in the final ballot?

5) What proportion of residents voted in favour of a TMO?

6) What are members views in surveys?

H   OTHER

1) Are committee meetings held regularly?

2) Are adequate minutes kept of committee and general meetings?

3) Are agendas sent out on time?

4) Are attendance records kept and meetings quorate?

5) Is the TMO office accessible to tenants, open at convenient hours and contactable in emergencies?

6) Has the TMO established clear procedures for dealing with the Right to Buy? (if responsible)

7) Has the TMO established an Action Plan for the coming year?

8) Will regular management reports on TMO business be produced?

Appendix 4

Roles of the Agency, Council and DoE

THE ROLE OF AN AGENCY

RIGHT TO MANAGE

ALL TENANTS' GROUPS wanting to develop a tenant management organisation with the support of Section 16 grant will have to appoint an *'approved agency'* to oversee the feasibility and development process. This agency also assesses whether your group is competent to do the job of tenant management.

Some of the jobs an *'approved agency'* must carry out are set down in the Right to Manage Regulations. Apart from these there are a number of other ways in which agencies can help you develop your TMO.

How much an agency takes on will depend on:

- ■ The skills and knowledge of your group
- ■ The support available from the council and other local workers
- ■ The staff the agency employs and their skills and experience

It is not necessary for *'approved agencies'* to carry out all the jobs involved in developing your TMO. Indeed, setting up a TMO works best where a partnership exists between tenants, agency and the council.

JOBS THE AGENCY MUST DO

APPROVED AGENCIES are responsible for:

- ■ Identifying what you need to know
- ■ Setting up a work programme
- ■ Arranging training

cntd.

- Evaluating training
- Assessing competence
- Drawing up the Management Agreement with your landlord
- Keeping tenants informed of your activities and plans

IDENTIFYING WHAT YOU NEED TO KNOW

YOUR GROUP MAY have a mixture of very experienced tenant activists, people with professional skills and newcomers. But everyone has useful skills and knowledge gained from their family or working life.

The agency should encourage everyone in your group to identify what skills and knowledge they already have and what training is required to help you to become competent to run a TMO. This is called assessing your training needs *(see Learning to Manage, Chapter 2).*

SETTING UP A WORK PROGRAMME

THERE ARE MANY more jobs to be done to develop a TMO than organising the right training. You have to apply for and administer a Section 16 grant, negotiate a management agreement with the council, provide information and consult with local tenants, set up an office and, if necessary, employ staff *(see Chapter 3).*

Approved agencies are responsible for agreeing a programme of work to achieve all these tasks, as well as agreeing a plan for carrying out the training you need. However, the agency need not carry out all the work themselves.

GENERAL ADMINISTRATION

DEALING WITH the administrative and organisational aspects of developing your TMO such as: venues for training and meetings; agendas and minutes for business meetings; travel and refreshments, may or may not be part of the agency's role. You will need to decide how much of this is sensible for your group or agency to deal with.

ARRANGING TRAINING

THERE MAY BE a number of local organisations who could provide some of the training in your programme. Although the agency is responsible for ensuring that you get the training you need, it may be more cost-effective to involve other organisations to carry some of this out.

If you use other organisations, the agency will be responsible for ensuring that the training meets your needs. The agency may work with local trainers, specialists, council staff and other tenant managers.

ASSESSING ESTATE PROBLEMS AND PRIORITIES

DURING THE feasibility stage the biggest task, for the agency, is to carry out an assessment of the estates' problems. This includes collecting information about the area and carrying out a tenants' survey.

EVALUATION OF TRAINING

ALTHOUGH YOU WILL have direct knowledge of how well a development programme is progressing, all agencies should ensure each training session and the overall programme is evaluated, at key stages in the development process.

The results should be discussed with you and a suitable solution found for any problems. *(See Learning to Manage, Chapter 4 for more on evaluation.)* A summary of your views on training will be sent to the Department of the Environment to help them monitor the quality of training.

ASSESSING COMPETENCE

AT THE END of the feasibility stage, and again at the end of the development stage, your group will need to show that it is competent. This means that committee members have the necessary skills and knowledge, that the group overall can show a range of abilities, and that the organisation has developed policies and systems.

THE MANAGEMENT AGREEMENT

YOU WILL HAVE to negotiate a management agreement with the council; setting out those functions and responsibilities your TMO will take over and those remaining with the council.

Your agreement will be based on the TMO Modular Management Agreement. Approved agencies are responsible for drawing up the agreement with you and the council *(see Chapter 4)*.

WRITING REPORTS

THE AGENCY has a duty to write a report on the Feasibility Study and the Development Programme. These reports are given to the TMO, the Department of the Environment and the Council.

DEMONSTRATING TENANT SUPPORT

YOUR GROUP WILL have to demonstrate support from local tenants for your activities and plans at the end of the feasibility and development stages.

Approved agencies are responsible for making the arrangements to test opinion through a ballot or poll. However, it is not necessary for the agency to actually carry out the ballot or opinion poll.

ROLE OF THE LOCAL AUTHORITY

THE LOCAL AUTHORITY has a very important role because the council owns the properties and has a responsibility for ensuring, that all tenants receive a quality housing service.

INFORMATION AND TRAINING TO TENANTS' GROUPS

MANY TMOs FIRST find out about tenant management from a local housing officer. Councils have an important role to play in providing information and training for tenants' groups so that they can become more fully involved in decisions about their estates.

cntd.

The *Training for Tenant Management* research found that over a third of councils already helped tenants' groups to get training and this number is growing.

SUPPORTING THE DEVELOPMENT OF TMOs

MORE AND MORE councils are supporting the development of TMOs. Some are doing so because they believe in the merits of involving tenants.

Others have supported development because they want to win funds to improve run-down estates. From April 1994, councils must allow tenants to manage their own areas if the TMO can show that it is competent and has local support.

CHECKING THAT YOU HAVE A VALID CONSTITUTION

ONCE A RIGHT to Manage notice is served, the local authority will check to ensure that you have a constitution that meets the model constitution criteria. This is an essential first stage in the Right to Manage process.

PROVIDE RESOURCES

COUNCILS HAVE a specific responsibility to provide reasonable financial and other forms of support for TMOs. This should include provision of office accommodation, training and facilities at appropriate points.

WORKING IN PARTNERSHIP WITH YOU AND THE AGENCY

THE TRAINING FOR Tenant Management study found that the development of TMOs worked best where there was a close relationship between the tenants, the agency and the council. In a partnership, everyone needs to be clear about their role and responsibilities. Councils and agencies also need to work in a way that suits your group.

PROVIDE INFORMATION AND ADVICE

COUNCIL OFFICERS should be able to provide a lot of information and advice about how the housing service is organised and how much it costs to provide. The local authority can also advise you on how the TMO's policies and systems will fit in with council policies and structures.

PROVIDING TRAINING

HOUSING STAFF may be able to provide training on the councils' existing policies and structures. It is also important that council staff, and councillors, are themselves trained about the role and responsibilities of a TMO. This will help the TMO and the council to work together.

One very useful training method is for tenants to spend time with housing staff, to see how they do their jobs. The council may be able to arrange visits to the repairs section, lettings office and other departments.

NEGOTIATE THE MANAGEMENT AGREEMENT

THE OPTIONS you choose in the management agreement must be negotiated with the local authority and agreed by the council.

CHALLENGING THE AGENCY'S REPORTS

THE AGENCY PRODUCES a report at the end of the feasibility and development stages on your progress. This will recommend whether the TMO should proceed. The council may disagree with the conclusions and decide to challenge these reports. If this happens the council may go to arbitration.

PROVIDE ALLOWANCES FOR MANAGEMENT AND MAINTENANCE

ONCE THE TMO is established the council will provide allowances for management and maintenance costs. These are negotiated with the management agreement along with arrangement for paying the money.

MONITORING PERFORMANCE

THE COUNCIL IS likely to want regular reports and information from your TMO once it is established. These will have been agreed in the management agreement *(see chapter 7).*

ONGOING SUPPORT

SECTION 16 FUNDING reduces once a TMO has taken over management and stops after the first year. The TMO is then responsible for meeting any training needs for committee members and TMO workers.

However, many councils will provide ongoing support and advice. Larger authorities, with several TMOs, often have a specialist section or member of staff who will help to sort out difficulties.

ROLE OF THE TENANT PARTICIPATION BRANCH

SECTION 16 GRANTS

THE TENANT PARTICIPATION Branch of the Department of Environment is responsible for promoting tenant participation and the development of TMOs.

The Branch also administers the Section 16 grant scheme which provides funds for training tenant managers. They receive and assess applications for grant aid and also monitor work carried out by Section 16 funded agencies.

The Branch are interested in ensuring training for TMOs is effective, of a high quality and provides value for money. If your group receives Section 16 funding, the Department will expect certain information about the training you are receiving and the costs involved.

APPROVING AGENCIES

THE DEPARTMENT 'approves' agencies for work with TMOs
if they pass certain tests concerning the quality of training and
support provided. A list of approved agencies can be obtained
from the Department of the Environment.

VALUE FOR MONEY

SUBSTANTIAL SUMS of money are spent each year on training
TMOs. The Tenant Participation Branch is keen to ensure this is
money well spent.

Part of their evaluation of training agencies involves looking at
the costs charged as well as the quality of work carried out. The
Department expects tenants choosing an approved agency to
also think about the costs of different agencies and whether
they provide 'value for money'. *(See Chapter 5.)*

*The range of services an agency can offer, and its all-round
expertise should be taken into account in assessing value
for money.*

EVALUATING TRAINING

THE TENANT PARTICIPATION Branch aims to make sure that
approved agencies continue to provide good support and training.
You will be asked to assess training sessions and this information
will be fed back to the DoE. You can also make complaints about
agencies to them if problems cannot be solved at a local level.

CHECKING THE MANAGEMENT AGREEMENT

AFTER YOU NEGOTIATE a management agreement with your
council this agreement must be formally approved by the Secretary
of State. The Tenant Participation Branch will handle this approval.

PUBLICATIONS AND RESEARCH

THE TENANT PARTICIPATION Branch also has a role in ensuring the most effective development of tenant management. It supports various research projects into tenant participation and TMOs and funds the development of books, manuals and videos to help TMO training.

Appendix 5

Approval of Agencies

INTRODUCTION

BEFORE THEY START to work with a TMO, agencies must be approved by the Department of the Environment. Agencies who are not approved cannot receive Section 16 funding.

The approval process is intended to ensure that agencies have a minimum level of competence to carry out their responsibilities towards tenants setting up TMOs. This includes their ability to assess training needs, organise work and training programmes and assess competence. In addition, agencies must assure the Department that they can exercise effective financial management and control.

ONCE APPROVED, agencies join a list of approved agencies. Agencies placed on the list will be continuously monitored by the DoE and will be the subject of regular full reviews.

Tenants' organisations can select freely from the list of Approved Agencies and are encouraged to invite several agencies to tender for work.

WHO CAN APPLY

AN AGENCY SEEKING approval may be an individual, a company, a partnership, a voluntary organisation, a housing association, a trust or some other combination of such organisations in a consortium. Agencies may be profit-making or non-profit making organisations.

The important thing is that the agency can demonstrate relevant experience and competence to take on the work involved in setting up a TMO.

HOW TO APPLY

AGENCIES ARE expected to demonstrate their competence in three ways:

- By completing a form setting out a calculation of the organisation's hourly charges (available from the DoE)
- By writing a report
- By attending an interview

THE REPORT

THE REPORT SHOULD be no more than 5,000 words plus appendices. It should be seen as an opportunity rather than an obstacle. This means that agencies can identify weaknesses and still receive approval if the Department is confident that steps are being taken to rectify them.

The report should contain:

- A brief introduction to the organisation, its aims, history and size
- Details of geographical area of operation (national, regional or local)
- Brief names and descriptions of key staff (with short CVs in the appendix including any qualifications and relevant experience)
- Staff development policy
- Equal opportunities policy
- Details of the approach taken to assessing training needs
- Details of the approach taken to training, including methods used, (with examples of course programmes or other relevant material on previous training experience in the appendix)
- Statement about ability to deliver (directly or indirectly) the key skills and knowledge identified and adopted by the Department as essential for tenant management
- Resources available, or normally provided by the agency (such as training equipment, handouts, booklets)

- Criteria applied to the selection of venues, training materials and other resources
- Procedures for quality assurance and / or quality control in training work, including details of how participants are given opportunities to provide feed back
- Details of the organisation's approach to assessing the competence of TMOs, including how gaps or weaknesses would be remedied
- Annual report and accounts for previous years (if available)
- Details of the fee structure, methods of calculating fees and typical charges

THE INTERVIEW

IF THE APPLICATION form and report indicate that the agency has suitable experience, the Department will arrange an interview with the agency's representatives. The agency will be expected to make a ten minute presentation, then answer questions.

The Department will try to give advance notice if any aspect of the application is causing concern or uncertainty.

The agency's representatives will be given an opportunity to ask questions. Interviews will normally last around 45-60 minutes.

AFTER THE INTERVIEW, the Department will reach a decision on the basis of the information available. Normally, agencies will be expected to meet all the criteria listed below. In the absence of one or two criteria, approval might still be given, subject to the condition that systems or staff, for example, were put in place. Approval could be made conditional on meeting the criteria, within a specified period of time.

In granting approval, the Department conditionally, or unconditionally, could comment on aspects of the agency's presentation or report. This might take the form of recommendations for change or improvement.

CRITERIA

THE CRITERIA show what the Department broadly expects
from agencies in relation to their competence as training
agencies. These criteria will be used to assist decisions
on the approval (and review) of agencies for inclusion
(and continuation) on the list of Approved Agencies.

The agency's report should show how the agency conforms
to the requirements set out in the criteria.

THE DECISION ABOUT inclusion (and continuation) on the
Approved List will be taken in the light of the information in
the report and other information submitted with it (such as
financial accounts and annual reports) or any other information available to the Department.

*Agencies will normally be informed of the reasons for the
refusal of their application for approval and which criteria
they were unable to meet. It is possible for an agency to
meet all the criteria but still not be approved because of
other factors taken into account - in particular the hourly
rate which the organisation would need to receive in grant.*

1 RELEVANT PREVIOUS EXPERIENCE

AGENCIES DO NOT necessarily need to have previous experience
of training or supporting TMOs, since that would make it impossible
for new agencies to become established in this field.

*Relevant experience could include training and supporting new
housing associations, ownership co-operatives, tenants groups,
and other community groups.*

Tenants who have established a TMO would also have relevant
experience. However, they would be expected to have had
some experience of training and supporting others before
being considered as Approved Agencies.

2 SYSTEMS FOR MAINTAINING QUALITY IN THE DELIVERY AND DESIGN OF TRAINING, INCLUDING SYSTEMS FOR MONITORING REACTIONS AND ASSESSING COMPETENCE

AGENCIES ARE EXPECTED to demonstrate that they have systems to ensure quality provision of training. This includes procedures for:

> → **Assessing training needs**
>
> → **Delivery or organising the delivery of relevant training**
>
> → **Assessing participants' views of training**
>
> → **Assessing competence**
>
> → **Reviewing and evaluating experience and**
>
> → **Managing the organisation effectively**

3 CAPACITY TO ENSURE DELIVERY OF AN AGREED PROGRAMME OF KEY TOPICS COVERING SKILLS & KNOWLEDGE REQUIRED FOR TENANT MANAGEMENT

THIS CAPACITY COULD be demonstrated in a number of ways, for example with reference to the previous experience of the agency and training materials used.

Agencies which propose to sub-contract some of the training to other organisation, should demonstrate that they can put together an appropriate training package and manage the sub-contractors properly.

4 STAFF WITH DEMONSTRABLE AND RELEVANT EXPERIENCE, SKILLS AND KNOWLEDGE

THE DEPARTMENT does not require any guarantees that particular staff would be available or designated to work on specific tasks. TMOs may want to insist that particular staff work with them and they are free to negotiate this.

cntd.

But some assurance must be provided that the organisation has key staff with relevant experience, skills and knowledge. There must also be procedures for staff development to make sure that expertise is developed.

Relevant skills and knowledge may show through details of staff experience, through qualifications or a combination of both.

There are no specific qualifications for training TMOs. However, relevant qualifications might include TMO competences, National Vocational Qualifications, the National Certificate in Tenant Participation, teaching qualifications, the Certificate in Community Work, the Certificate of the Institute of Training and Development and professional housing qualifications.

AFTER APPROVAL

AFTER AN AGENCY is placed on the approved list, the department will monitor its performance through the submission of quarterly financial returns and six-monthly progress reports, including summaries of tenants' views of training.

In addition, the Department makes monitoring visits from time to time. There are proposals to supplement these with more systematic assessment visits carried out by independent assessors. Their job will be to ensure that the criteria used in approving the agency are being met in practice and that the information provided by the agency in its regular progress reports is well founded.

IF THIS MONITORING gives rise to serious concerns, the Department may remove the agency from the list. This would usually be preceded by a written warning. If the concerns are less serious, specific conditions may be laid down for future performance.

The agency's position on the list will be reviewed at regular intervals. This will be done by a process broadly similar to the process for approval described above, with the difference that the Department will draw on the agency's experience of working with TMOs.

Example Brief
Inviting Tenders from
Approved Agencies

Any Estate Tenants Organisation
44 Any Town Flats
High Street
Any Town

x February 199( )

Dear _____

DEVELOPING TENANT MANAGEMENT ON ANY ESTATE

The **Any Estate Tenants' Association** invites you to submit a detailed proposal to act as their *'approved agency'*, assisting in the training and development of a Tenant Management Organisation (TMO). We attach a copy of the Right to Manage notice which was accepted by Any Town Council on *x February*, and a copy of our constitution.

Background

Any Estate Tenants' Association has been working with council support staff for six months considering the future of 750 houses in the *xxxx district* of Any Town. After a period of training for the group, an information campaign and series of public meetings were held on the estate. A majority vote of our members, held on 30 January, supported our proposal to investigate the idea of tenant management further.

Aims and Objectives

We are keen to take an active part in improving conditions on our estate. Our aim is to improve local housing services and create a better community spirit amongst local residents, by exploring the idea of a TMO on our estate.

The Estate and its Tenants

Any Estate lies to the Northwest of Any Town. It has 750 houses built in the 1940s. Once a popular and thriving area, the estate is now difficult to let. The estate is managed from a neighbourhood office some two miles away. Despite frequent promises, planned improvement programmes to windows, kitchens and heating systems have yet to be carried out. Problems with vandalism, dogs, crime and poor social facilities have led to low morale amongst tenants. Unemployment on the estate is currently $x\%$ and there is a concentration of elderly people and families with young children.

Recent Developments

With help from a local neighbourhood workers and the tenant liaison section of the housing department, a group of tenants have recently come together to look at the problems on the estate and seek solutions. The council has recently signed a Tenants Charter and is generally supportive. They have given us a small grant (£200) and some training in committee work. We are the first tenants' group to consider managing our own homes, in the district.

Next Steps

The group are now ready to carry out a feasibility study into the benefits of setting up a Tenant Management organisation. We need help to:

* Examine the options and decide whether tenant management is what we want

* Get a basic knowledge of housing management and finance

cntd.

* Get more people involved in the group and keep tenants informed
* Organise a ballot
* Prepare for the development stage if we decide to go ahead with a TMO

Timetable

We hope to appoint an agency to start work in April for a period of 6-9 months. We require your submission by 5 March. Interviews for shortlisted agencies will be held on 17 March.

Information to be Provided

In addition to detailed proposals on how your agency would work with us, we also need:

* General information about your agency and the work it carries out
* Details of the staff who would work on this job, their qualifications and experience
* Details of your total fee, hours involved and hourly rate
* References from two previous clients

Please submit your proposals to the above address, for the attention of _____ by 12 noon on 5 March.

I look forward to hearing from you,

Yours sincerely

Secretary
Any Estate Tenants' Group

Appendix 7

Example Person
Specification for Agency
Workers

DUTIES & RESPONSIBILITIES **A**

Promote tenant participation

Promote tenant management

Identify Estate problems and priorities

Develop training programmes to suit tenants' needs

Work in partnership with the local authority

Work with office bearers to develop specific skills and knowledge

Work with tenants' group to develop team and committee skills

Assess competence

Arrange ballot

Provide training on:
TMO responsibilities
TMO policies
TMO rules and constitution

Section 16 grant regime

TMO finance

Financial Control

Employment of staff

Office procedures

Housing management

Housing legislation

Repairs and maintenance

Negotiation skills

Equal opportunities

KNOWLEDGE REQUIRED **B**

What TP involves

What TMOs involve

How councils work

Housing legislation

Housing finance

Housing management

How to identify training needs

Training methods

Organising meetings

Producing newsletters

Public speaking

Rules and constitutions

Committee work

Management agreement

TMO policies

Section 16 grants

TMO finance

Financial control

Recruitment

Employment law

Staff management

Office procedures

Repairs and maintenance

Caretaking

Evaluating training

Performance monitoring

cntd.

SKILLS REQUIRED

Communication
Public speaking
Team building
Assertiveness
Negotiation
Motivating
Facilitating

Listening
Counselling
Planning
Time-management
Self-awareness
Administrative skills

Dealing with difficult situations
Financial skills
Interviewing
Computer skills

ATTITUDES REQUIRED

D

Commitment to tenant participation
Positive view of TMOs
Non-discriminatory
Non-judgemental
Honesty

Flexibility
Self-motivated
Determined
Confident
Desire to increase skills and knowledge

Importance of good performance
Importance of independent viewpoint
Importance of accountability

Appendix 8

FURTHER INFORMATION

This *Guide* refers to a number of other publications which you will find useful. These are listed below.

- CATCH (1993) *The Employment Handbook* CATCH
- Chandler, H. (1991) *The Right Information* PEP
- DoE (1989) *Tenants in the Lead* HMSO
- Institute of Housing (1993) *Housing Management Standards Manual* Chartered Institute of Housing
- Rodgers et al (1994) *Modular Management Agreement for Tenant Management Organisations* HMSO
- Scott et al (1994) *Learning to Manage* HMSO
- Scott et al (1994) *Preparing to Manage* HMSO
- M. White (forthcoming) *Managing the Money* PEP

Finally, an address which you will certainly need is:

Tenant Participation Branch
Room N10/05
Department of the Environment
2 Marsham Street
London
SW1P 3EW

Printed in the United Kingdom for HMSO Dd 0297768 3/94 C20 3400/4 280525 10/29457